THE BOOK OF YOU
(AND ME)

JOEY ESSEX

THE BOOK OF YOU
(AND ME)

HODDER

First published in Great Britain in 2015 by
Hodder & Stoughton
An Hachette UK company

First published in paperback in 2015

1

Copyright © Joey Essex 2015
Illustrations © Damien Weighill 2015

The right of Joey Essex to be identified as the Author of the Work has been
asserted by him in accordance with the Copyright, Designs and Patents Act 1988.

All rights reserved. No part of this publication may be reproduced, stored in a
retrieval system, or transmitted, in any form or by any means without the prior
written permission of the publisher, nor be otherwise circulated in any form
of binding or cover other than that in which it is published and without a similar
condition being imposed on the subsequent purchaser.

A CIP catalogue record for this title is available from the British Library

ISBN 978 1 473 61629 5

Typeset and designed by Craig Burgess
Illustrations by Damien Weighill and Ben Summers (pages 209, 211, 242)
Printed and bound by CPI Group (UK) Ltd, Croydon, CR0 4YY

Hodder & Stoughton policy is to use papers that are natural, renewable
and recyclable products and made from wood grown in sustainable forests.
The logging and manufacturing processes are expected to conform to the
environmental regulations of the country of origin.

Hodder & Stoughton Ltd
Carmelite House
50 Victoria Embankment
London EC4Y 0DZ

www.hodder.co.uk

This book belongs to ....

My favourite page is ....

I am Reem because ....

INTRODUCTION

Alright, my friends, what are YOU sayin'? It's me again. With a whole new book. Welcome to the second chapter in my life as 'Joey Essex: the author of books'.

I wonder if one day in the future these books will be used in studies about how young men in Essex used to live their lives? Maybe I'll be talked about in the same way we talk about dinosaurs, and professors will try and work out why Joey Essex became extinct. Or maybe someone will find this book all mouldy in a corner of a street a million years from now and it will have turned into a book fossil. A bossil.

For those of you who read my first book – *Being Reem* – this one is going to be *very* different. The last one was all about my life, but this one is more about what mad strange things go on in my brain. If I had to look inside my brain to see what ingredients were in there I think there might be some broccoli and a bit of porridge. So be warned: Things might get weird.

And as you know, my first book was the only book I've ever read from start to finish. So this one will be the second book I've read start to finish. But the best thing about this one is that you, my fans, will be helping me fill it. Because this book isn't just about me – it's about YOU and me. What are YOU sayin'? This time I'm not even joking, I really want to know!

Throughout the book there will be pages or gaps for you to fill in with your own thoughts and ideas. I also want you to draw pictures in the book where I've asked you to. The other brilliant thing is that on some pages I've put a hashtag so that you can take a shot of it for me and tweet it or Instagram it so I can see what page you're on and then it will be like we're reading it together.

Here's a little rap I've written to get you in the book reading mood:

This is my book
You don't want to know how long it took
I'm not Jamie Oliver, no I'm not a cook
If you get rude you will get shook
So you might want to have a good look
In some of the nooks
You won't find any hooks
(because then you would hurt yourself and I'd get sued for injuring people who read my book).

How to USE THIS BOOK

You should read this book in any order you feel like. If you always hate page 100 (maybe you're allergic to the number 100?) then skip page 100 and go to page 102. You can literally jump about wherever you want. There are no rules. Read it from back to front if you feel like it. YOU make the rules! You'll find loads of stuff in here that probably makes no sense to anyone, but might make a lot of sense to someone... and that's kind of the point.

You can find out how I'd survive in the wild (I'd make friends with the bears for a start) on page 86. You can see how I'd answer some seriously difficult headscratchers like 'what came first: the chicken or the egg?' (I should have just asked someone at Nando's that question, I'm sure they'd know.) Or you can draw your dream house and then see if it looks the same as mine (page 170). And if, like me, you can't ever face going to the cinema on your own because you get bored, or scared, then just read my film reviews instead (page 74) and then you don't need to bother!

There's also a chapter where I answer some of the dilemmas you tweeted me a few months ago (page 152) and another one where I promise I'll follow twenty people who send me some amazing fascinating facts.

I have such creepy sick fans and I want you all to be part of this book, and mostly I just want us to have some fun.

So this is for you AND me.

Joey x

BUY A FUNNY POSTCARD TO USE AS A BOOKMARK.

When you've finished the book write
a review of it on the postcard and
send it to your local bookshop.

GO AND FIND THE BEST PLACE
TO FLY A KITE...AND THEN
FLY ONE!

I've started a flipbook in the corner of this page.
Now you carry it on throughout the whole book!

Diary of Joey's weekend.

HERE'S A TYPICAL WEEKEND IN ESSEX FOR ME:

Friday:

Weekends are different than they used to be. Friday nights
don't count as weekend anymore because there's not much going
on – there's no hype about them. So sometimes a Wednesday in
Essex is better than a Friday. I usually call them Wednesday
Weekends!

This Friday I got my mates round – Dan, Jamie, Mitch & Steve –
to have a conch in the crib. This meant they just sat on my sofa
and talked sh*t while I ended up sitting on the floor. I don't know
why I always sit on the floor when I have loads of seats in my
lounge! But for some reason I like the corner of the carpet by
the coffee table and the settee. When I was a kid I always liked
sleeping on the floor. I was what you might call a 'floor dweller'.

I was meant to cook for everyone, but I didn't. I really want to
be able to cook lasagne but it's too hard so we ordered an Indian
takeaway instead. I used to get chicken korma but now I get

16

chicken tandoori and spinach with rice because I'm being healthy. We watched *Home Alone* on telly (although I definitely wasn't home alone). We chatted about everything. Our friendship means we're so close that we can just talk about whatever we want. We take the p*ss out of each other, but it doesn't matter. If I'm ever upset about anything I can tell them, but I'm in a good place at the moment. I'm not in a soppy mood these days. I'm on top of the world!

I was so tired that I fell asleep before everyone else and they had to let themselves out. I woke up on the floor at 3am and had to get into my bed before I turned into a piece of carpet.

Saturday:

I woke up at 9.30am, then went back to sleep until midday. I'm getting really good sleep at the moment. I'm having deep dreams and feel really happy. I love waking up on my own and being able to play about on my phone in bed by myself.

I was going out into town in the evening so I had to plan my outfit for the night out. Problem is at the moment I'm going through a bit of a stage where I don't know how to dress. Well, I do know how to put clothes on – otherwise I'd be walking around naked – but I'm at that middle age, twenty-four, so I don't know whether I should dress smart or casual. I'm trying to be grown up in a dress sense mode but I'm not grown up. I'm quite stupid.

Tonight I wore chunky leather boots, which I got in Australia, black skinny jeans, a really fitted white shirt (I've been doing loads of exercise recently and people have said they can tell my shoulders have got bigger). I had a long black leather jacket on and looked like I was in *The Matrix*. At least I hope I did, otherwise I looked like one of Westlife.

Me and a few mates went to the W Hotel in the West End, had a little party and bumped into some girls I'd met in Ibiza when I was twenty. They're quite salty potatoes. There were two girls who were trying to chat to me and one of them was really annoying. She was quite fit but rude. When I was talking to her mate she kept jumping in front of her and I thought 'what are you doing?' It was really cringy so I told her to stop doing it. I needed to have my own space and she was too full on. I don't usually go out looking for a girl; I'd rather have a chat with my mates.

I haven't made up any new dance moves for a while but my new thing to do in clubs is to walk through the crowd with your head down... I call it Ranging, which means you dive through the crowd like a worm.

We went home about 2.30am. I didn't drink too much because it stops you being able to talk to girls and they think you're an idiot.

Sunday:

I woke up at 9.30am again. My mate Dan and his girlfriend Katie stayed over in the spare room. We ordered pizza for breakfast (you're allowed to do that on a Sunday) and I watched *Home Alone* again. I usually feel guilty eating bad stuff but I didn't feel too bad because it's hangover food. And you do need to treat yourself a little bit. We stayed in the house all day and they left about 3pm.

I don't like my own company much because I feel like I'm missing out or wasting my life. So after they went I watched *Home Alone* again. Can you tell it's my favourite film?

WHAT DID YOU DO THIS WEEKEND?
WRITE A DIARY ENTRY ON THIS PAGE:

What's under my bed?

I'm usually very tidy and don't have anything under my bed, but sometimes I let things fester like a Jester. That means I build up a bit of a collection of stuff from my life before I tidy it up and start again.

This week I've got a bit of a build-up. Here's what I've found under my crib.

SOCKS: Inside out obviously. I always wear my socks inside out because I don't like the creases on my skin.

A COWBELL: I won this when I came first on *The Jump* on Channel 4. I meant to put it on the wall but I'm waiting to put it in my dream house. And I have to build that first. I keep treading on it by accident when I wake up and it makes a loud noise. When I first won it I thought I had to buy a cow if I had a cowbell, but that won't fit in my house. If I did buy a cow I'd probably call it Craig: Craig David.

21

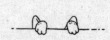

SLIDERS: I wear these all the time instead of slippers.

WEIGHTS: For me to build my muscles in the morning.

A CRYSTAL SKULL: It used to be in my living room but it's broken so I chucked it under the bed. Only the ghosts can see it now.

A PLATE WITH BAKED BEANS ON: They've gone a bit furry now.

A VERSACE CHAIN: That's where it is! I thought I'd lost it!

A POWER RANGER OUTFIT: I can't remember where I got it but I've been saving it for a fancy dress party at my house. I just haven't had the party yet.

A RUBBER DUCK: I think it knows I've started to like squirrels better so has gone to hide.

TIME YOURSELF DOING THE ACTIVITIES BELOW,

And then try and beat your own time!

Running up the stairs

Building a tower out of twenty marshmallows

Speed walking to the nearest postbox

Eating five cream crackers

Saying the alphabet (forwards and backwards)

Doing a handstand

Swimming ten laps of your local swimming pool

Speed read a book

Making an omelette

Tidying up your bedroom

WRITE A POEM FOR SOMEONE YOU CARE ABOUT.

Here's a poem about my cat Prince:

I love you Prince you're my cat,
You don't live with me now but you used to live in my flat
It was dangerous and you used to fall out of the window...
   (Seriously he did... he'd open the window and crawl out of the
   side of it. But that doesn't rhyme. Let me start again...)
It was dangerous for you and my flat stunk like poo and now it
   smells really nice,
And I'm sorry I'm leaving you for five weeks to go on the ice
   (when I went on *The Jump*),
I always visit you and you're getting really big,
You're not a mole and you can't dig,
   (I've got a video of him looking like he's a mole)
Your leopard stripes are still insane,
When you had that fight you must've been in pain,
I don't know what goes on in your brain,
You can't drive in the fast lane...
...So take it slow.

Your poem here:

 Tweet me a picture of your poem.

Joey's Headscratchers

WHAT CAME FIRST: THE CHICKEN OR THE EGG?

This is a very strange question to ask anyone. You're probably wondering why I've got it in this book. And I wouldn't recommend you going up to a girl or boy you fancy and saying it as a chat-up line. Well, unless maybe they really like chickens or eggs.

Apparently this is a question that loads of clever fellas always discussed — and they kept arguing about it for years. I'm not really sure why they cared so much about eggs. Maybe they were hard to come by in those days. Maybe they'd never had a fried egg sandwich before.

If you ask me what came first: the chicken or the egg? I'd say it would be the egg. Because without the egg how did the chicken hatch?

But then you start thinking about it more and it gets even more confusing because the egg would've had to have been laid by a chicken. So then how did the chicken get here? Personally I think God probably laid the egg because he does everything, doesn't he?

Apparently one of the first blokes to start bothering about this question was a guy called Aristotle (who lived in 384–322 BC which is AGES ago) and he reckoned both the bird and egg were about at the same time, so none of them were first.

This is what he said:

'If there has been a first man he must have been born without father or mother – which is repugnant to nature. For there could not have been a first egg to give a beginning to birds, or there should have been a first bird which gave a beginning to eggs; for a bird comes from an egg.'

I don't know what the hell any of that means. But forget about the egg for a minute, Aristotle sounds like quite a cool geezer. I reckon he was a scientist. He wore thick glasses and had wonky teeth and a bald head. I think he wore white shirts too.

Stephen Hawking got in on the chat after that and started telling everyone that the egg came before the chicken. Stephen Hawking is the one in the wheelchair with the voice simulator. And the cleverest man in the world. He says the same as me about the egg, so I think we're quite similar.

I don't know which side he was on though. I'd be team egg more than team chicken if I had to choose a team.

Hang on, think about this. If an elephant laid an egg and a lion came out of that egg – would it be an elephant egg or a lion egg? I'd say it would be an elephant egg because he owns it. Although someone could have shoved the egg up his bum!

Then there's someone called Charles Darwin, who I thought was the president. But turns out he's not. He wrote something about the 'Theory of Evolution' which I think is about how we came from monkeys. And I think he means that anything could come from anything so you'll never know whether an egg or a chicken was first. Which is all a bit deep.

I like to think Charles wore a blue jumper and had quite a long neck. He's got his ears pierced for some reason and he wears really tight jeans.

Adam and Eve must have had something to do with all of this stuff too. I reckon Adam went 'Look there's an egg, do you want egg on toast?' and Eve said 'Nah, just leave it.'

Adam and Eve created the world (although I used to think it was Richard and Judy). The story of how it happened is really weird but I reckon they look quite normal, really old fashioned and Roman looking. Sometimes people show pictures of them in books and they look naked but the Adam and Eve I like to think about have got trousers on and he's wearing a sleeveless jumper. He's quite a smart guy, but a bit boring. Eve's OK, she's quite a sort.

I don't really remember the story about how the world started but I think there was an apple involved. And I think Eve threw it in a pond or something. Eve was a bit of a cow like that.

Anyway I don't know why we're talking about apples now. It's all about the egg.

But what about chocolate eggs?

It's quite confusing why we get chocolate eggs for Easter, I never understood it. Someone must have said 'Let's have a chocolate egg!' – and that must've had something to do with the chicken and the egg.

It's a bit too much for my brain.

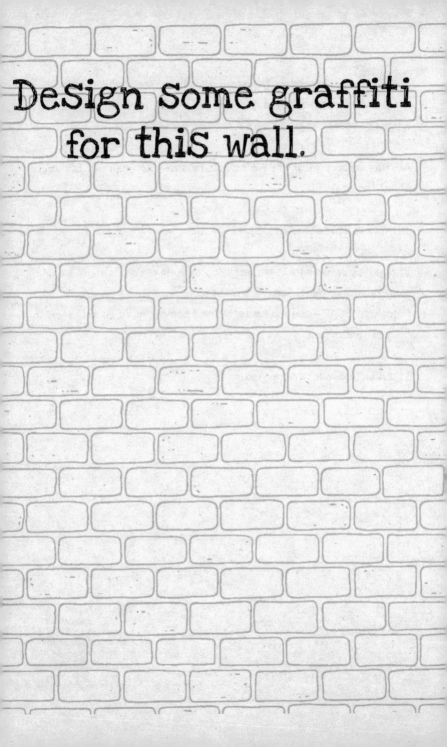

Design some graffiti
for this wall.

REEM ST.

JOEY'S JOKE BATTLE

I'm not very good at remembering jokes. To me when something is 'jokes' it means it's well good. Or chooong (which is better than good, because it's chooooooong).

Here are some jokes I think are *jokes*. I've given you my answer and the actual answer. See if you can come up with a better punch line. If you can, then you can officially change your name to 'Jokes McGee'.

Q: What's brown and sticky?
Joey: Rice
You: ....
A: A stick

Q: What do you call a three-legged donkey?
Joey: A donkey with three legs
You: ....
A: Wonky
(Wonky is actually a better one to be fair.)

Q: Knock knock
Joey: Go away, I'm on the toilet
You: ....

Q: Why can't your nose be twelve inches long?
Joey: Because I'm not a liar
You: ....
A: Because then it would be a foot

Q: What do you call a camel with no humps?
Joey: A horse?
You: ....
A: Humphrey

Q: What do you call a bagel that can fly?
Joey: A UFO
You: ....
A: A Plane Bagel
(Plane Bagel. Now that *is* jokes)

Q: A man with carrots in his ears walks onto a bus, the driver
says 'Why have you got carrots in your ears?'
Joey: Because I couldn't find any ear-plugs, mate
You: ....
A: The man says 'I can't hear you. I have carrots
in my ears'

33

Q: What did Zero say to number eight?
Joey: You're double of me
You: ....
A: 'Nice belt'

Q: What do you call a boomerang that doesn't come back?
Joey: A see-ya-later-rang
You: ....
A: A stick

Q: Where are otters from?
Joey: New York
You: ....
A: Otter Space

Q: Why does Snoop Dogg carry an umbrella?
Joey: Because he's allergic to the rain.
You: ....
A: Fo' drizzle.

GROW A CRESS HEAD!

What you need:

CRESS SEEDS
AN EGG (OBVIOUSLY!)
KITCHEN ROLL
COTTON WOOL
FELT TIPS OR PAINT
SCISSORS

How to make your cress head:

After eating a boiled egg clean the inside of the egg gently, so it doesn't break. Now draw a face on the egg.

When the face has dried, wet some kitchen roll and put it in the bottom of the egg shell. Next wet some cotton wool and put it on top of the kitchen roll. Make sure there is a gap between the cotton wool and the top of the egg shell.

Put some cress seeds on the cotton wool and press them down gently. Put your egg shells or pot in a sunny, warm spot.

When the cress gets green leaves on top of the stalks, you can eat it! Cut the tops off the stalks and try them in a sandwich or a salad.

My Morning Routine
BY JOEY ESSEX

MY IDEAL TIME TO GET OUT OF BED IS ABOUT 9.30AM.
I'm pretty good in the mornings, I never usually
struggle unless I've got a hangover and then
I always think I've got puffa fish face. I
need about seven hours' sleep to stop the puff.

Someone once told me you could put cold tea bags on your eyes to
get rid of the puffy bags, but that's just weird. Wouldn't you have
a smelly orange tea head?

THE FIRST THING I THINK ABOUT WHEN I WAKE UP IS PORRIDGE.
I love it more than anyone else in the world. I'd like my own
brand of oats. Essex Oats.

I SPEND AGES LOOKING AT TWITTER before I get out of bed. Usually just at what my mates or people I know have been up to. To see if they've been out. Next it's Instagram. There are so many girls on there! I've just looked at a picture from ages ago when there was a dog on *Britain's Got Talent* that hypnotised Ant and Dec and made them think they both have a tiny willy!

THEN I'LL LOOK ON WHATSAPP. I've got a group with my mates. We'll just ask who wants to go to Nando's or someone will send a stupid picture of one of us with a girl to wind each other up.

I GET UP AND CLEAN MY TEETH. I normally clean them in the night too. I wake up in the middle of the night, go to the toilet and clean them a few times. I must get through a lot of toothpaste. I think a ghost touched my foot in the night the other night. Maybe it was telling me I needed to clean my teeth.

I'LL GO TO THE MIRROR AND PULL FACES or talk to myself.

I'll say: '*I know you're tired but you've got to go and do this TV interview. Get on with it and we can chat later*'

THEN I'LL ACTUALLY MAKE MY PORRIDGE. I'll put a big handful of oats into a saucepan and put some coconut milk in there. Whisk it around for 3–4 minutes, put it into a bowl, pour some honey on and a chopped-up banana. I love it so much that sometimes I'll have it for dinner too.

I ALWAYS MOISTURISE my whole body after a shower. And I moisturise my face twice before I go out. I don't know why, I think it's going to keep my face quite fresh for when I'm older.

WRITE DOWN SOMETHING THAT YOU ARE GRATEFUL FOR EVERY DAY THIS WEEK...

Monday
Today I am grateful for...

Tuesday
Today I am grateful for...

Wednesday
Today I am grateful for...

Thursday

Today I am grateful for...

Friday

Today I am grateful for...

Saturday

Today I am grateful for...

Sunday

Today I am grateful for...

DRAW WHAT YOU'LL LOOK LIKE WHEN YOU'RE NINETY YEARS OLD...

I think I'm a good age at the moment because it means I can date girls of twenty-seven or twenty-eight but also younger ones, like twenty-three. I worry about getting to thirty. But in a way I'm excited. I've heard that when you're thirty, life becomes really, really weird and cool. And your body changes and it all becomes well good. Someone told me that. Unless I dreamt it.

Apparently you start seeing things differently in your brain and it becomes sick. But I'm scared about it. I think it might be like a weird dream where you start flying through space.

God knows what I'll look like when I'm ninety! But here's what I reckon...

walking stick!

Me... Jes Espex Age: 90

I'd quite like silver hair. I sprayed it silver when I was doing *Educating Joey Essex* and was trying to become a model. I think it would suit me but I'd have to tell Phillip Schofield so he doesn't think we're the same person.

In the picture I've got a walking stick, but it looks more like a block of wood. My walking stick would talk to me – like in James Bond – and it would change colour to match whatever outfit I was wearing. It would be a Walking Talking stick.

SHOW ME WHAT YOU'RE GOING TO LOOK LIKE WHEN YOU'RE NINETY BY DRAWING A PICTURE BELOW:

MAKE A NEW TWITTER FRIEND AND WRITE DOWN YOUR CONVERSATION HERE

FIND DIFFERENT OBJECTS TO JUGGLE WITH

(nothing sharp or dangerous
like sharks or rocks!)

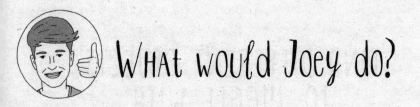# What would Joey do?

If you had a magical power to choose between two things happening to you, which would you pick?

1. You lose your right foot.
2. You lose your left foot.

I'd definitely lose my left foot, because my right foot is more useful. I can kick harder with my right foot and that's handy for when I want to play football. But then again I'd only have one foot, so it might be hard to kick anyway because I'd be hopping about.

Whether I had one foot or not, I'd still make sure I wore nice shoes. I'd make them extra special because I could only wear one of them at a time. God, it would be looong, wouldn't it? Because every single pair of trainers you bought would have a spare left trainer hanging about. I'd have to make sure I could get half-price trainers all the time. Or I'd have a special shelf with all my left-footed trainers. I know! I'd find someone else who had lost their right foot so we could buy trainers together!

Actually if I *really* lost my left foot I'd get a fake foot. In fact, I'd get loads of different sick feet that I could swap about. One of them would have loads of tattoos all over it and when I got bored of them I could just swap it. I'd have one that's completely gold. One that's got an ankle watch already attached. I'd get one that's tanned for when I go on holiday so it means I don't even need to bother sunbathing with it. And another that's really small so I can trick people. I can say to people 'Did you know I have a really small foot?' and they'll look down and my left foot will be tiny, like a size two. While the other one will be a nine.

OK, next dilemma. What about if you have a magical power to stop one of these things happening?

1. You lose your voice.
2. You lose your hearing.

I think I'd have to pick my hearing because at least then I wouldn't get headaches. I'd use the vibration of my voice in my head to work out what I was saying to people. And I reckon I'd be good at lip reading, so I'd work out what everyone was talking to me about.

If I couldn't hear any more though... how would I dance to music? I wouldn't know what to do. I'd rather just lose one ear and a little bit of my voice. So it's just a bit quieter than normal and I can't shout anymore.

47

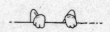

Next one: Which one of these would you do?

1. Forget all the good things that have ever happened to you.
2. Forget everything that ever happened to you.

That's a bit of a trick question. You have to just forget the good things. Otherwise if you choose number two then you forget the good things anyway.

I wouldn't really want to forget the good things though – because that would mean I'd forget the times I cut my mate James' hair with scissors, the time I realised I was a fantastic skier on *The Jump*, the moment I saw a stick insect for the first time in *I'm a Celebrity ... Get Me Out of Here!* and the time I created my Fusey haircut. Tough one.

You can choose to have no money, or no friends ... what do you pick?

I'd say no money. Money doesn't buy you happiness, that's one thing I've learnt in this business. Or maybe I can just find a friend who's got loads of money and they can treat me to Nando's.

Floyd Mayweather wouldn't say that though. He's a boxer and he says 'Some people say money can't buy you happiness, well look at me!' and he's got a jet and about twenty Ferraris. He's got so much money he doesn't care about anything. He's head of the money team.

What about this one then...

1. You develop an illness where you have to repeat your every
   thought out loud.
2. A girl you like says everything she thinks out loud.

I'd love it to happen to the girl. It would be perfect! Then I'd
know if she fancied me or not. But if it was me I'd hate people to
hear what I was thinking. I'd have to stay indoors. I'd never go
out, I'd sit in and talk to myself all the time because I couldn't be
around anyone else.

MAKE UP SOME NEW CHAT-UP LINES

I don't usually like chat-up lines. They're the worst things in the world to use. I just say 'What's your name? I'm Joey Essex'. Having a surname like Essex usually helps you talk to people. But some fellas I know try using lines to chat girls up. One geezer told me the weirdest chat-up line the other day... it was something about farting:

'Does it smell over here, babe? Because I was standing behind you a minute ago and you blew me away.' WHAT?!

Here are some others I've heard before:

You look like a parking ticket because you've got 'fine' written all over you.

Are you Jamaican?
'Cos you're Jamaican me crazy

Do you have any raisins? How about a date then?
I'd say no because I don't like raisins

I lost my phone number, can I borrow yours?
That's quite a good one to be fair

Fat Penguin! (WHAT?) I just wanted to say something that would break the ice.
I like that one too – OK, maybe lines aren't so bad!

If you were a bogey, I would pick you first.
I'm not sure that would work on ANY girl!

If you were a McDonald's burger ... you'd be a McGorgeous.

Are you Swedish? 'Cos you're the SWEEDISH girl in the room!
Sweetest, get it?

If you were a tropical fruit, you'd be a Fine-apple!

Do you like salt?
Do you like potatoes?
Well guess what, you're a salty little potato.
And she'd probably walk off and say 'you're cringing me out'.

Can you do any better? How would you chat someone up? Try and come up with your own new chat-up lines here.

Joey's Top Ten Essex Destinations

My flat in Woodford because it's a cotch.

Which basically means you can cotch in it. It's jammin', really comfortable.

Sheesh restaurant in Chigwell.

It's a lovely big restaurant and you can cotch in there and eat chicken and lamb. It has the nicest food ever. The whole of Essex goes there. It's a restaurant bar. Problem is you'll probably end up seeing your ex in there!

Sugar Hut in Brentwood

You can party there and have a good time, and Mick's always there. He's a nice guy. He's good for advice and sometimes he sorts me out with champagne.

Fusey. My shop on Crown Street in Brentwood.

It's the best clothing shop in Essex. Gemma Collins has a shop nearby, but I haven't been to it yet. I'm not there enough. I

probably go to Fusey once every three weeks, but I still have
a say in what clothes get stocked. I go to the buyers and pick
what's what.

Chigwell Park

It's pure memories and you can play football there. Sometimes
I go on the swings. It's jokes.

The brook

You can make base camps and look for ducks. Although you're
more likely to see foxes instead. I used to go to the brook all the
time when I was a kid.

Nando's in Loughton

I'm in there all the time, I think I must be their best customer.
Nando's always send me chicken cheques so I can get free food.
I don't think the chickens actually write the cheques, but it
would be jokes if they did. When I go there I always get a whole
chicken, medium hot sauce, sweet potato mash and two perinaise
sauces. They do chilli jam in there too apparently, but that sounds
weird. Actual jam with chilli in?

Chigwell station

Because you can get straight to central London very quickly.
If you try and drive from Essex it can sometimes cause
AGGRAVATIIOOOON. And that's loooong.

Faces nightclub

We used to film in there a lot for TOWIE. It should be called Boats because that's the word for if you've got a face around town. I might start a club called 'Joey's Boat Race'.

Queens Road in Buckhurst Hill

It's a good all-rounder. They've got a lot of hairdressers, shops, a Waitrose and places to eat. If you don't know what to do in Essex go there and you're sorted.

PRANK CALL SOMEONE
WHO WON'T MIND...
LIKE YOUR DAD, BROTHER,
SISTER OR BEST MATES.

FUSEY IS MY BRAND,
NOW I WANT TO SEE YOURS.

Design a logo for your own brand.

VISIT A MUSEUM OR AN ART GALLERY AND WRITE A REVIEW HERE.

Instagram video your trip

START YOUR CHRISTMAS LIST

...and keep adding to it throughout the year.
So you don't forget.

ANIMAL FIGHTS

Some animals make weird friends with each other — like I saw a picture of a bird with its wing around a rat once. And a chimpanzee cuddling up to a tiger. And did you see that weasel riding the woodpecker? Mad.

But friendships are boring. Let's work out who would win if they had a fight.

Monkey and a rabbit

The monkey would win, he'd throw bananas and the rabbit wouldn't be able to do anything because he doesn't use his hands, all he does is nibble carrots.

Woodlouse and a tortoise

The woodlouse would curl into a ball and roll away... so really the tortoise loses because he's so big in comparison and should've seen it coming.

Snail and a fox

The snail could pretend to be a rock and then the tortoise from the other fight (with the woodlouse) would decide to join this fight and he'd pick up the snail and throw it at the fox, and the fox would fall over. He'd be really embarrassed that he'd been beaten up by a tortoise AND a snail.

Pig and a penguin

This is a hard one. Pigs are meant to be clever, but they look disgusting. If it was me – Joey Essex – against a pig the pig would win because I'd go to touch it then run off to wash my hands. I know they're meant to be really clean but they look dirty [I've got a whole lot of pig chat for you on page 82]. I know I'm not meant to be involved in this fight because I'm not an animal, so I think the penguin would beat the pig with its wings and win.

Spider and rat

The spider would wrap a web around the rat. And maybe after it could tickle it to death, because apparently rats laugh when they're tickled. But who would want to tickle a rat and test it out?

Baboon and a barn owl

The baboon would get its bum and fart into the barn owl's mouth and the owl would run off as fast as possible. The baboon also has a really red bum so the owl would need glasses from staring at it.

Otter and a prawn

The otter would beat the sh*t out of the prawn, wouldn't it? I know the prawn has a lot of armour because of its shell, but don't they eat poo for a living? So that's not good. Prawns are the wimps of the sea. Sea otters hold hands when they sleep to keep from drifting apart. That's cute, innit?

Alligator and a dog

The dog will live in a house so it can easily escape back to its cotch. If it was my dog it would be alligator trained so there would be no contest.

I used to watch films with alligators in – or was that anaconda? Wasn't Jennifer Lopez in that one?

Squirrel and a snow leopard

The squirrel, because it would run up a tree and start pelting the snow leopard in the head with acorns. Squirrels have worse memories than me; they plant loads of new trees each year because they keep forgetting where they put their acorns.

Turtle and a slow loris

Have you ever seen a slow loris? Look on YouTube... they like being tickled. They're like little monkeys or mini bears and put their hands up when you tickle them. I really want one. They're so jokes. I think in this fight the turtle would probably win by tickling the slow loris with his head and then would retreat into his shell. Guess what, turtles can breathe through their bums. How mad is that?

Dolphin and a guinea pig

Dolphins are the strongest and cleverest animals in the world. Dolphins have names for each other too. That's how cool they are. They know how to fight because they beat up sharks in groups. So if they beat up sharks surely they can do a guinea pig? Guinea pigs are pointless, they're like rubbish versions of rats. And they can't decide what to do with their feet either because it's like they've pinched them from a bird.

Elephant and a hamster

You'll be surprised with my answer to this but I'm going to go with the hamster. I had a hamster once and it was so fast I couldn't catch it when it came out of its cage. So I think the hamster would probably run up the elephant's bum and live in his body and start annoying him so much the elephant would just give up and never talk to him ever again.

Seahorse and a real horse

Horses are a bit wimpy but seahorses are amazing. Plus real horses don't know how to swim so they'd lose. Seahorses are cute because they mate for life, and when they travel they hold each other's tails.

Goat and a bear

Paris Hilton had a goat once and tried to smuggle it onto a plane. That's a bit weird. Goats are good at climbing mountains and really steep surfaces. If anyone ever tells you you're walking like a goat that's a compliment. But the goat doesn't have much chance in this fight because it's up against the mighty bear. Sorry, goat. And guess what? There have been studies that show that goats have accents like we do. Although that study might just be someone trying to wind me up to be honest.

Giraffe and a gorilla

The giraffe would wrap its long neck round the gorilla's head and win. And the gorilla might think 'this is a nice scarf' and not realise it's being had.

Panda and a cow

The panda wouldn't mess about and would probably just throw a pie or some bamboo in the cow's face. The cow would be scared. Did you know a newborn panda weighs as much as a cup of tea? And I read somewhere that cows have best friends and spend most of their time together. How anyone can actually work that out I don't know. It must be one of those myths. How does anyone actually know whether a cow has mates? I'd like it if they did though. I'd be able to show them my cowbell.

MY HEROES
BY JOEY ESSEX

Batman

He's got a lot of swag. He's got a black cape and is all blacked out. I like the fact he keeps his dignity and no one knows who he is.

My cat Prince

Or Catman as I sometimes like to call him. He's not a man, he's a cat, but he's very honest and he always tells the truth. Even though he can't officially speak because he's a cat.

My dad

Who's a human, not a cat. He's the person I rely on most in life. Although sometimes family is annoying I love him. He's taught me to always stick up for myself, to be generous and always be nice to girls. I want to grow up and be like my dad. Everyone says I'm going to look like him, but he's quite big these days. He finds it hilarious and winds me up saying I'm going to look like him one day if I eat too much. I can always phone him and ask him for advice. I would say he'd be good at advice for everyone but I think he only gives me advice because he cares about me. He's very on the ball and never lets me get into debt. If my car insurance was coming up in three months' time he'd be on the phone now to remind me to do it.

My mate Steve Cass

Steve is very good at keeping secrets. I can talk to him about everything and he won't say anything. I see him the most out of my mates. He's honest and truthful, a bit like my cat Prince. He'd tell me if he thought I was being an idiot and I'd listen to him. But usually we're in situations together, so if I was being an idiot then he's probably being one too!

Mrs Copper

She was one of my teachers at school and sat next to me in every lesson trying to help me concentrate. I admire her for trying so hard to teach me something I knew I'd never learn. I did try to tell her but she wouldn't listen. I'd love to meet her again.

My agent Dave

He's a sort of hero. He's like my cool hero. He'd look good in a cape. He's just had his teeth done extra white so they're really powerful and could probably blind someone in a fight. That could be his superpower.

Can I put myself on this list?...Oh. No. The editor of this book has just said I'm not allowed...

Keith Lemon

He's my hero because he can become so many different people.
That's his superpower. I've never seen someone so good at
impressions!

WHO ARE YOUR HEROES?

Think about it carefully and write them down here:

WHERE HAVE YOU BEEN?

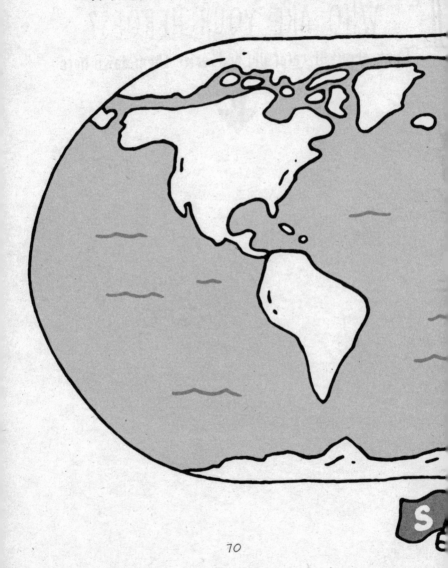

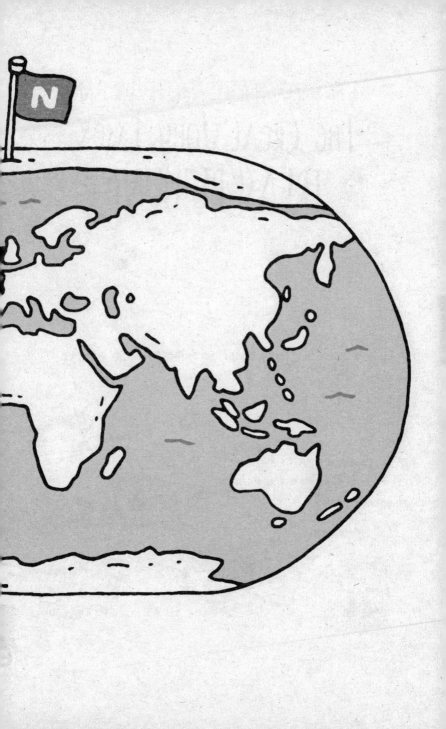

The Great Joey Essex
Treasure Hunt

Find all of these items:

A four leaf clover
A perfectly round pebble
Two left shoes that look almost the same but different
A Nokia 8210
A signed copy of this book
A rainbow cupcake
Porridge
A Supersoaker water gun
The funniest word in the dictionary
A sponge football

DRAW A FILM POSTER FOR THE MOVIE OF YOUR LIFE.

Who would be in it?
Who would play you?

JOEY'S FILM REVIEWS

I can't sit and watch a film on my own because I think it's weird.
I want to have someone with me so we can talk about it and I
can get their opinion on the film. I could never ever go to the
cinema on my own! I'd be so freaked out. And bored. But I've
watched some films especially for you. If you've never seen
these films then now you don't have to ... if you have, then did you
think the same as me?

The Wizard of Oz

I remember watching this when I was
a kid and thinking 'wow' this is all so
advanced. When I'm older my kids will
probably look at the things I've watched
and think 'You're so ancient', whereas
I think it's all modern now. And now
when you look at this film it's so old and
strange. It starts in black and white and then goes into mad
colours like the telly doesn't know how to transmit the colours
properly. There's a yellow road that they all seem to really like
for some reason, and some really short people who like munching

SILVER
MAN

things. The munchkins. There's a main girl who has some red shoes that she taps to get her home (I'd quite like some shoes that could take me to places), a lion, a scarecrow and a silver man. I liked him the best. My sister was scared of the witch. They're all after a meeting with some wizard who lives in a green town. Back then if you'd asked me I'd have given it 8 out of 10... but now I'd give it 1.

Back To The Future

I loved this film when I was a kid. There's a guy in it who is really cool. It is such a sick film. I think Keith Lemon has the actual outfit from the film that he's bought for himself and wears to parties. The guy has a time machine that takes him to meet his mum and dad before they got together. Michael J. Fox is the guy's name in real life, which is a cool name too. It's set in 1985 and then he goes further back, but I wasn't even born in 1985. That's mad. When I was a kid I always dreamed I lived in space. I loved gadgets and I loved frogs. Imagine meeting your parents before they'd had you and having a chat with them? I'd love to meet my dad when he was my age. It's so annoying that you can't do that. I'd give *Back to the Future* a 7 out of 10. Because it's got a car in it and a man with mad hair.

Mary Poppins

My dad likes the woman in *Mary Poppins* who's also in *The Sound of Music*. I can't watch it though; I'm not a fan of musicals. In this film she's much fitter, she looks better with dark hair. It's

funny watching it thinking that she was the same sort of level of fame at the time as someone like Angelina Jolie now. And now it's only older people who really know who she is. This film is about a nanny who lives on a cloud and then comes and looks after some kids and sings a lot. My sister loves films like this but I could never sit and watch it the whole way through. I haven't got the attention span. My score: 4 out of 10. *Mary Poppins* is a bit of a sort though. I'd take her out for dinner. But her singing would annoy me.

Indiana Jones

He was a cowboy, wasn't he? Or a professor or something, but basically he wears a cowboy hat so that means he's a cowboy. He goes into a tomb and runs away and there are a few snakes. And he whips things. Are there places like that in real life? I think there are. He looks like he's wearing eyeliner. He runs about a bit; he's not really a superhero but he's a brave guy. My rating is 3 out of 10.

Dirty Dancing

My sister was well into this sort of stuff and still is. She always used to try and make me watch it. It's sad knowing the main guy Patrick Swayze is dead now, it makes me feel horrible. But at least everyone still fancies him in the film. His dancing is quite cool. I'd like to dance like him. The lead girl has got a stupid name though – Baby. Why's she called Baby when she's clearly not a baby? And then he moans about her being put in the corner or something. He sings a song about hungry eyes. How can you have hungry eyes? Imagine eating pizza out of your eyes. That would be weird. Joey's rating: 6 out of 10.

Grease

I love this film. I always wanted to look like Danny Zuko. It reminds me of what I reckon my dad was like in the olden days. Boys trying to be all cool to impress the girl. Sandy's a bit geeky but he still loves her. 9 out of 10.

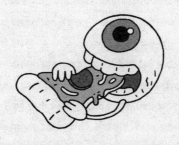

MY PERFECT PIZZA

I'd normally only have a pizza if I've been training really hard for three or four weeks, and then the boys would come over and we'd order a takeaway. But I've heard you can make your own pizza in a healthy way by using cauliflower as the base and once I learn to make that I'll eat them every day.

I love ordering a really massive pizza and then being able to come back for more, like a buffet. It's even better when it's cold and you eat it the next morning. Some people have it with salad cream but that's weird. I have it with barbecue sauce.

My ideal pizza would be made with mushrooms, sweetcorn, meatballs and a barbecue base. If you place the ingredients carefully enough you could probably make it to look like someone's face. Someone like Louis Walsh. But that might put you off your food a bit.

It would need to be proper chooooooouunnng which means bare nice, pepperoni and I'd call it a choooung meat turner.

DRAW WHAT WOULD BE ON
YOUR PERFECT PIZZA...

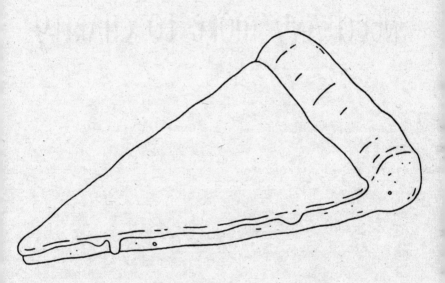

Give something you don't
need any more to charity

COME UP WITH YOUR OWN CATCHPHRASE LIKE...

LOOK REEM, SMELL REEM, BE REEM.

Joey's Headscratchers

DO PIGS HAVE FEELINGS?

Pigs are weird things, aren't they?

I'd like to think they have feelings, but they can't have... like can they fall in love? If you ask me I don't think pigs can have feelings because if they cared about anyone they would clean themselves... and they stink.

Someone told me the other day I've been wrong about pigs. Apparently they're like the fourth cleverest animal in the world, cleverer than dogs. But I ate a pig's brain when I was in the jungle on *I'm a Celebrity... Get Me Out of Here!* and I didn't get any more brainy. So what's that about?

This is what I've heard about pigs. It will blow your mind.

Pigs are really sociable and while they sleep they love to cuddle up close and sleep with their noses touching. Nose to nose. If humans did that we wouldn't be able to breathe, would we? Or we'd catch loads of colds.

Pigs also greet other pigs they know by rubbing noses in the same way we shake hands.

Pigs dream like humans do. I reckon they dream about sausages – but that would be a nightmare.

Pigs spend hours playing, sunbathing and exploring. Some people who have worked on farms with pigs have said that they've seen them listening to music, playing with footballs, and getting massages.

Pigs are freaks, man. I reckon they listen to dirty house music.

Pigs have about twenty different ways to communicate with each other and different oinks mean different things like 'I fancy you' to a pretty pig they've seen cotching in the mud nearby. Or a different type of oink saying, 'I'm hungry!'

Some professor reckons that pigs have more brainpower than a human three-year-old. (And Joey Essex probably.)

Adult pigs can run at speeds of up to 11 miles an hour.

Someone did an experiment once and saw pigs could play video games! They use their snouts to operate the joystick and got 80 per cent of the game right!

We should never say that people 'eat like pigs' because actually in real life, pigs eat slowly and take their time over their dinner. So we have been giving them a bad rep. We've had a bad impression of them because they seem like dirty little pink freaks. When actually they're nice.

Pigs don't gobble up their food like dogs, instead they nibble and sniff at it to decide whether they want to eat it or not.

Hang on, I do that!
Maybe I was a pig in another life.
Piggy Essex.

Pigs are really clean too. They might look like they're well dirty but they always keep the place where they sleep tidy and don't go to the toilet in it. Pigs don't 'sweat like pigs' either because they can't sweat.

They actually prefer water to mud. One woman built a shower for her pigs, and they learned to turn it on and off by themselves!

Pigs have feelings and are usually very happy, but like humans they can sometimes have a bit of a bad day and think to themselves 'what have I done wrong?' Pigs are sensitive and emotional and can get depressed like we do. I guess this answers my question!!

So eating a pig is like eating your dog! They're too clever and nice for us to turn them into sausages and pork sandwiches. This is what Cameron Diaz said after she heard that pigs have the same brain power as a three-year-old human:

'[Eating bacon is] like eating my niece!'

Pigs have good memories, they can recognise and remember up to thirty other pigs. Did you know that pigs have a good sense of direction and are able to find their way over long distances?

Pigs come to their own name just days after they've been born!

There was a story about a pig that lived in New Zealand once and it used to sing at the moon. She was famous in her town and all the school children used to come and give her tummy a rub and she would sit and listen to songs when people played them on the beach. She liked violin the best.

This all sounds like a load of bullsh*t I know. But it's true. I might go and watch *Babe: Pig in the City* again now I've seen pigs in a different light. Although that one's a bit weird because it talks.

I wish pigs didn't look so dirty because then people might be nicer about them.

I could buy a micro pig but I don't think my cat Prince would like it.

JOEY'S SURVIVAL SKILLS

I reckon I could easily be one of those explorer survival people.
Like that fella Bear Grylls. Imagine I've taken over from him
and no one watches him on telly any more. I'd need a new name —
maybe 'Bear Long'.

Everything about me would be long because I'd been living in the
wilderness for a long time. So I'd have long hair, long fingernails,
and I've already got long legs and well long fingers. People always
say my toes are massive too.

But what would I do? Where would I sleep? What would I wear?

I think I'd wear a Peter Pan sort of outfit, green skinny jeans
(but they'd be ripped), a camouflage cape, a green top and a
green cowboy hat. So I'd be half Peter Pan and half Indiana
Jones. I would have learnt how to crack whips like Indiana Jones
so I'd definitely have a whip with me, that would sound sick when
I'm flying through the trees on a mission.

I'd have a metal cup so I could drink from it and cook stuff in it.

Bear Grylls has drunk his own wee before, which is disgusting. If I HAD to – because there was no water – I probably would drink my own wee, but I'd hate it, I'd be soooo pissed off. Literally. Because it would be piss.

Did you know that humans can't survive if they go more than three days without water, but they could survive for several weeks without food?

So that means you probably would have to drink your own wee... sorry.

Here's some survival questions from Bear Long to test how long you'd be able to survive in the wilderness:

Which water source is the cleanest?

- O River
- O Lake
- O Spring
- O Pond

The answer is spring. I guessed it right but I thought it was just because it sounds fresh. Spring's quite a good name for a kid, isn't it?

'Spring Essex'. I might call my son or daughter that if I have one. Or maybe 'Autumn'.

Here's another one. What should you do if someone you know gets stung by a jellyfish?

- O Ice it.
- O Soak it in hot water.
- O Rinse it with cold water.
- O Wee on it.

I always thought you're meant to wee on them, because that's what you always see on TV – I think it even happened in *Friends* once and Chandler wees on Monica on the beach. But I just looked it up and apparently the right answer to this question is 'soak it in hot water'. You're meant to remove the tentacles using tweezers, a stick, or a credit card (how would you use a credit card?!). Anything but your hands, otherwise you'll keep getting stung. Then soak it in the hottest water you can stand.

But I'd still wee on it.

Here's what Bear Long would have in his survival kit man bag:

- O Swiss army knife
- O Socks
- O Boxers
- O Some rope

I might take a tampon too because I know how to light a fire with one of them (I did it when I was in *I'm a Celebrity*).

But what would I eat?

I know it sounds harsh but I'd have to start killing chickens. I'd have to, wouldn't I? The thing is, if you chop off a chicken's head or wring its neck – which is meant to be how you kill them – then they still run around for a few seconds with no head on! That's where the saying 'running around like a headless chicken' comes from. Some other animals can do that too – like a turtle, which can carry on swimming for a bit even with no head. It's something to do with their body being pre-programmed to work even without a head!

That's mad, innit?

I wonder what would happen to a human if we didn't have a head? Would we carry on walking about? I don't think we would.

And apparently if you give rice to a pigeon it blows up.

And what's that thing about cats having nine lives? I think it's because they can fall and jump from massive heights and should really be dead afterwards but they just walk away as if there's nothing wrong with them.

What if I met an actual bear in the wilderness and I was called Bear Long?

I'd have to become one of them so they didn't eat me. I'd have to make friends with them. You can become mates with tigers and bears. Have you ever seen this video about the Harrods lion? Someone bought a lion from Harrods years ago and lived with him in Chelsea for a bit. He was called Christian the lion. Then they released him into the wild and when they met him again nearly a year later he started running at them and hugged them! It's amazing. It's on YouTube. It's quite emotional.

So I'd try and find some bear cubs and I'd be their mate, feed them chickens and chat to them. Then they'd get bigger than me and they'd be feeding me and killing stuff for me. I'd be the king.

King Bear Long.

DESIGN YOUR OWN EMOJI

DRAW WHAT YOU WOULD WEAR ON YOUR FIRST DAY AT WORK.

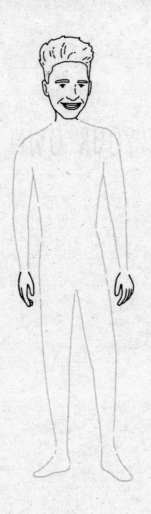

MAKE A SANDWICH

...using only ingredients that you have in your kitchen cupboards. Write down what you used.

CREATE A NEW DANCE MOVE AND GIVE IT A NAME.

Try it out next time you're in a club.

 Instagram video your move

WRITE A FAN FICTION STORY ABOUT YOUR FAVOURITE FAMOUS PERSON.

PETS IN COSTUMES!

I reckon pets love being dressed up in costumes, and I think
my cat Prince could carry off most things. So I've given him a
selection. The cape and the hat are well sick. Even though the hat
picture makes him look like he doesn't have a face.

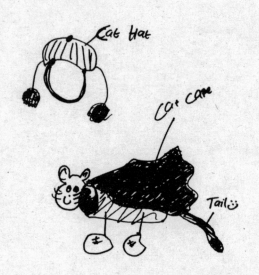

WHAT COSTUME WOULD YOU PUT YOUR PET IN? DRAW IT HERE.

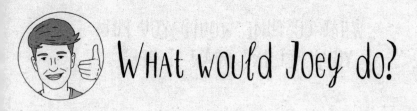

What would Joey do?

If you had to choose out of these, what would you do?

1. You always look young, but get old really quickly.
2. You always look old, but you live longer and age slowly.

I'd have to pick the first one. There's that saying 'We're here for a short time not a long time'. Or is it 'We're here for a good time not a long time...'?

When you think about it life isn't that long anyway. I religiously live by the word YOLO – you only live once. I always want to enjoy myself. If I can't be bothered to go out then I say to myself 'You only live once'.

I need to make the most of my twenties because I've had to come to terms with the fact recently that when I'm thirty I'm going to have to settle down and get married.

Next dilemma:

1. You are the last person left on Earth.
2. You are the first and only person to live on a new planet.

I would DEFINITELY pick the second one. I'd love to be the first person on a new planet, wouldn't you? I'd be like Adam and Eve but I'd be Joey Essex. I'd have to make sure I didn't throw the apple in the pond this time.

I reckon I'd find a button that would teleport me to this new world whenever I wanted. But then the question would be, would I tell people about it or not? I'd have to be really picky about who I spoke to. I'd have a special move I'd do with my hands that would get me into the new world.

I'd have to choose who I told wisely. I'm quite wise I think. I'd get my dad involved. And Steve Cass. I might bring my agent Dave but he'd probably try and take it over and sell it. Or he'd bring loads of journalists.

How about...
What do you choose?

1. Dogs become extinct.
2. Cats become extinct.

The answer is dogs. Otherwise Prince wouldn't be in my life. And cats are more G than dogs. They have more swag. I can say I've got my own leopard! And dogs are more aggressive.

What about this...

1. You lose your toes.
2. You lose your thumbs.

I'd say my toes because they're quite horrible anyway, and I could just put trainers on and pretend I had toes.

OK, what if...

You're on a date with a girl or boy you don't like and you want to get out of it, what do you do?

This has happened to me a few times. I've been out with a girl and just thought 'I can't be here anymore'. So I've pretended that I think everyone's looking at me in the restaurant and that I'm getting all paranoid and I'll say to her 'Crap! I need to get out of here'.

There was once a girl who I hung out with and I knew I didn't fancy her but she was cool so I liked being with her. I did tell her at the start 'You'd better not fall in love with me.' And she said 'I won't'. But then a couple of months later when we were out and

I was chatting to another girl she started screwing and crying at me. She kept saying 'You can't just speak to other people' and I told her 'I don't like you like that'. And we never spoke again which was a shame. It was probably my fault for being close with her. But I did tell her not to fall in love with me!

When it comes to lying, the best excuse for anything is that one at school when people say 'My dog ate my homework' – although mine would have to be my cat because I don't have a dog. That ACTUALLY happened to my mate Tom Pearce. His dog really did eat all of his coursework once! When he told the teacher they didn't believe him. The dog must've been extra clever after that.

HAVE YOU EVER NOTICED...

that there are some funny names for things. Here are some I think are really weird...

ZIP - (OK, this is one i've made up) is a special recipe that I created. It's couscous with avocado and onion, and then you sprinkle on some special oil that I call voodoo oil. I think it's called Udo oil. It's been recommended by scientists and doctors that it's the best oil ever in the world to eat.

CARROT - that's quite a weird word. You don't ever use that word normally. Like no one is called carrot, are they? But then no one is called onion or broccoli either.

TOAD IN THE HOLE - that's another odd one. It sounds horrible – why would you want to eat a toad? – but it's a nice dish. I fancy it now actually.

SHEPHERD'S PIE - what's a shepherd got to do with a pie?

LASAGNE - a weird one too. I'd just call it cheesy squared pasta.

BUBBLE AND SQUEAK - that's just leftovers.

SPOTTED DICK - that's a sponge with raisins in. When would you EVER dare order that in a restaurant? Eww.

WELSH RAREBIT - is basically cheese on toast. So what that has to do with rabbits I don't know.

BLACK PUDDING - I thought it was made of beetroot, but it's pigs' blood. Now I know all about pigs and how clever they are I think I'll swerve it.

CAULIFLOWER - could you call your daughter Flower? Or Cauli? It's not really much of a flower. You wouldn't put a cauliflower in a vase on your table, would you?

STINKING BISHOP - that's apparently the smelliest cheese ever. And it sounds like it. I don't eat cheese anymore because it gives me weird dreams. If I have cheese I wake up screaming in the night. It's like going on a rollercoaster. If I want to have a weird night I could say 'I'm not going out tonight, I'm just going to have some cheese'. It's like a crazy night out.

TRY TO IMPROVE YOUR MEMORY
BY USING THESE TIPS AND TRICKS.

Get organised...

Did you know that you're more likely to forget things if your home, bedroom or office is a mess? I've been told that making a list is a good way to remember the things you've got to do.

Get some sleep...

For your memory to be working at its best most adults need seven to eight hours of sleep a day. Obviously it's hard at the weekends and when you're busy, but try and get into a routine, that'll help too.

Doodle...

Apparently people who doodle have better memories, so this whole book should help improve your memory! Experts say doodling helps us to concentrate and stops us daydreaming, too. Doodle all over this page if you want to!

Get some exercise...

It's been proven that exercise can boost your memory and brain power. Twenty minutes of exercise before an exam can improve how you do. So go for a walk and ace your exams... easy!

Turn off your phone...

Apps, Twitter, Instagram are wicked, but try having a day when you don't use your phone and instead you just concentrate on what's going on around you. Rather than taking photos to remember things, maybe write them down in this book.

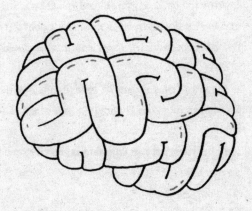

MY BUCKET LIST:
THINGS TO DO BEFORE YOU DIE

I think it's called a bucket list because you can fit all the stuff you want to do in a bucket.

Here's what's on my list:

1 I'd like to climb the Eiffel Tower like Spiderman.

2 I want to buy a jet pack and fly about. I'd probably just fly around Essex. I think it would be cool to fly to Sugar Hut and fly to the roof. Everyone would think I was Father Christmas.

3 I'd like to get a massive sledge filled with cushions and put all my mates in it and fly down a mountain.

4 I'd like to meet the Queen and have a chat – this is what I'd say to her:
'Do you get fed?'
(Apparently she gets fed by special people who test her food.)
I'd also ask her:

'What's it like being such a boat?'
(A boat is a face, a famous person, and
she's the biggest boat in England. She's
also a G – a gangsta.)
I'd say:
'What's it like having your face on
every single note in the country? And
can I have my face on a five pound note
please?'
Then I'd ask:
'What's your actual job? How do you make your money?'
(She must have done something! Her job is basically just to wave
at people. I'd hate that. My hand would hurt. She's on Twitter –
I think she follows me, but that might be a fake queen.)

5 I'd like to be in a really cool Hollywood film where one minute
I'm on the road starving hungry, lost in the desert trying to
survive... actually that doesn't sound like a very funny film,
does it? Then I'll see a cactus and cut it open with my door
key. I'd get Leonardo DiCaprio to play me in the
film about my life. I think he'd make a good
me. But it depends if he has the minerals.
Has he got it in him? Has he drunk his
Berocca? Has he 'got game'?

6 I'd like a beach house in loads of hot places but I would rent
   one. I wouldn't bother buying one because the only reason
   I'd have it would be to take girls there. And then each one I
   took would moan and say 'Didn't you take your last girlfriend
   there?' so it would be a waste of money. Miami, Hawaii,
   Barbados... I'd have one everywhere.

7 I'd like to try a deep fried pizza or a
   Snickers bar but I think they only do
   them in Scotland?

8 I'd eat in a restaurant in total pitch
   black. There's one in London called
   Dans le Noir and you're served by blind
   waiters. I am definitely doing that. But it'll
   be hard if I need to try and find the toilet.

9 Buy a stranger a cup of coffee. As long as they like coffee.
   If not they can have a hot chocolate.

WHAT WOULD BE ON YOUR BUCKET LIST? MAKE YOUR LIST HERE.

HIDE SOMETHING FOR A FRIEND
TO FIND AND DRAW A MAP TO
IT ON THE NEXT PAGE.

DRAW YOUR MAP HERE!

DRAW WHAT YOU WOULD WEAR ON YOUR WEDDING DAY

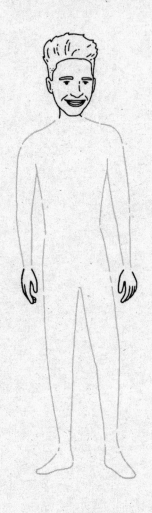

Learn how to do a Handstand.

Joey's Headscratchers

CAN YOU DIE OF A BROKEN HEART?

I reckon you can you know. Your heart races when you're thinking about someone and you think you're having a heart attack. I've thought I've had heartache before when I've been in love. It's weird.

I've heard of stories before where there was an old woman and an old man who had been married for about fifty years and when the man died, his wife died about a week after him. That's sad, isn't it? But also quite nice because it means they weren't apart for very long.

I think there's actual science to prove it. There's a thing called broken heart syndrome.

Do you think love comes from your brain or your heart?

Sometimes my brain will tell me what the right thing to do is, and it will tell me if I fall for a girl it might hurt at some point... but I still go with what my heart says. I always listen to my heart more than my brain.

Can love make things taste nicer?

Yes. When you love someone they always smell good and food tastes a hundred times better. But if you really don't fancy a girl then it makes the food taste disgusting and you don't want to eat it.

How long do you reckon it takes to decide whether you fancy someone or not?

Someone told me it takes four minutes to fall in love. But I think about seven minutes. Here's why:

MINUTE 1: You're thinking 'she's got something about her'

MINUTE 2: You greet her and you hear her voice and it's nice

MINUTE 3: You start having a bit of a conversation and she tells you her name and you think 'that's a nice name'

MINUTE 4: You're talking properly

MINUTE 5: You're thinking, 'I quite like this girl, I might ask her out'

MINUTE 6: Your heart's going and beating 100 miles an hour

MINUTE 7: You ask her out and she says yes and then you're IN LOVE

But then again there's a Take That song that says it only takes a minute to fall in love. So who knows who's telling the truth...

Maybe it's Gary Barlow after all.

And apparently (according to scientists and people who know this sort of stuff) you fall in love seven times before you get married. Which is quite a lot when you think about it. I've got quite a long way to go that means. And what about the poor girl who ends up being number seven? I'll have to say to her, 'Sorry, mate, I've got to say goodbye to you because it's all about number eight. Laters, it's all about Miss Eighters'.

I think people fancy people who look the same level of attractiveness as them and they're the ones they end up marrying. Although not if that means they look exactly like you. I wouldn't fancy someone who looked just like Joey Essex. That would be weird.

Also men who kiss their wives in the morning are meant to live five years longer than men who don't. So I'd be well old because I always kiss girls in the morning ;-)

If I had to choose between an attractive face OR a nice body I'd have to choose body. But actually, if I was going to marry that person they'd need to have a pretty face because that's what I'd have to look at for the rest of my life across the pillow in the bed.

So maybe it's the face. The Boat race. The boat.

And did you know you're more likely to fall in love with someone if you stare straight into their eyes?

Well, as long as they don't just think you're trying to have a staring contest anyway.

PARTY TRICKS

The only party trick I do is called 'Dragon fingers'. I created it to stop people asking me at parties what I could do that was different. Because now I can say 'I can do the dragon'. This only works though if you have really long fingers like me. (My fingers are extra long.)

○ You put your hands together like you're praying

○ Then spread your fingers out

○ Then you fold your wedding fingers over each other

o Then you tuck your finger behind your middle finger into your
   index finger...

o Then you make a little mouth and it becomes a dragon

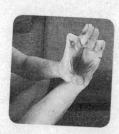 

Girls aren't normally all that impressed though, I think they just
think I'm a bit weird.

My mate Charlie just breakdances when he gets to parties.

Party tricks are pointless though really because at a party you
should be enjoying yourself not doing tricks.

EAT EVERY DIFFERENT TYPE OF QUALITY
STREET IN THE TUB, REVIEW THEM AND RATE
THEM IN ORDER OF BEST TO WORST.

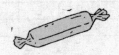

FIND ALL OF THESE WORDS:

REEM DUBAI JUMP VERSACE

FUSEY ESSEX MARBS

PRINCE JUNGLE JOEY

T	J	N	J	L	W	F	B	Y	L
S	C	O	Z	P	R	I	N	C	E
A	E	R	J	K	A	N	L	V	S
Y	A	M	E	H	P	U	R	E	S
F	W	P	V	E	X	S	Z	R	X
U	M	W	L	B	M	G	V	S	R
S	A	J	U	N	G	L	E	A	I
E	R	U	V	R	U	D	G	C	P
Y	B	M	Y	L	S	I	H	E	Q
B	S	P	H	O	D	U	B	A	I

DRAW A MOUSTACHE ON YOUR FACE AND GO TO THE SHOPS WITH IT ON.

 Tweet me a picture @JoeyEssex_

HERE'S SOME NEW HAIRSTYLES I'M GOING TO TRY OUT...

I like to stay versatile like Versace. Versoose.

The first one would be a ponytail for boys, but three of them. It won't be a pigtail or a ponytail, it will be a triple tail. It will be made up of corn rows and will have one in the middle, and then you can clip one to the left-hand side. It will start from the top and come all the way down.

So the names of my new signature styles are:

The triple tail

Fusey
  (OK, that's an old one but still a good one)

The icloud

...WHAT HAIRSTYLES DO YOU THINK
I SHOULD TRY? DRAW THEM ON
THE HEADS BELOW.

JOEY'S FAIRYTALES
(JOEYTALES!)

If someone said to me 'tell me a fairytale' the first thing I'd say was 'is it about a fairy?' But then I'd realise that fairytales are about magical mad stories that don't really exist. Problem is, I can't actually remember what happens in any of them. But I'll try my best...

Snow White

I thought this was about the girl who loses her shoe, but I've just been told it's not. So here's what I think Snow White is about:

Snow White is really pasty, she's never been in the sun in her life. She lives in the snow in an igloo and she wears a butters dress, it's horrible. She's not actually pretty at all, she's got dirty hair and needs a wash. She also needs a tan. She just dances a lot and then one day she gets into breakdancing. Well if it was my story that's what she'd do anyway. I'd make her learn some decent moves to make her a bit cooler, to give her a bit more street cred. I think there were some dwarves about somewhere too but not sure what they were doing. Who's the girl who gets lost in the maze and goes to a mirror asking about who the fairest is of them all? Is that her too? There's a witch in it somewhere who's jealous of her. And I think she marries a prince. Although not my cat, that would be very odd. I don't think cats can get married.

Cinderella

She's well fit, *she's* the one with the shoes. She loses it and is fuming and wants to get a new pair. Then I come along – Prince Joey – and get her a new pair and she says 'sweet'.

Red Riding Hood

This is the story of when the wolf comes to a girl's house and nicks her clothes. And he takes her money. He goes into her house, comes out wearing a red hood, runs about, thinks he's it, and then he gets robbed by someone cool like me who gets her clothes back and also her money. And she falls in love with him (me) and we get married.

The Gingerbread man

He was the thief. He was naughty. It's a bit stupid being a thief when you're made of gingerbread. Because people want to eat you. And you haven't got any muscles.

Sleeping Beauty

Every time she slept she got more beautiful and then she got so pretty her head exploded. Is that what happened?

WHY SHOULD I FOLLOW YOU ON TWITTER?

Write down the reason and tweet it to me.

Take a selfie with your postman!

CREATE A NEW GAME. WRITE DOWN THE RULES,

DRAW WHAT IT WOULD LOOK LIKE AND WHAT YOU'D NEED TO PLAY IT.

CUSTOMISE A PIECE OF CLOTHING TO MAKE IT **FUSEY**.

Joey Essex:
PARTY PLANNER

If I was planning a party for my mates here's the key
ingredients to make sure it's creepy sick:

○ Indoor swimming pool
○ Floaters – like lilos but with a better name
○ Water pistols – good to flirt with girls and get them in the hair!
○ Cocktails
○ Champagne (champagne cocktails maybe!)
○ Equal amount of girls to boys – but I'd have to have the
  fittest bird
○ Outdoor barbeque – with steak burgers and sausages
○ Game of Twister
○ A trampoline
○ I'd also have my own band who would rise from the floor
  whenever I wanted some music. Maybe the perfect band I've
  created on page 184.

WHAT WOULD YOUR PARTY BE LIKE?
WRITE A LIST OF YOUR PERFECT
PARTY INGREDIENTS HERE.

WHAT ARE THE
CLEVEREST ANIMALS?

Octopus

They're quite strange sticky things, aren't they? In a million years' time they might not even exist. I think they have such large brains which is why they're up there on the clever animal scale. Apparently scientists keep discovering stuff about octopus, like they've found out they can solve problems and have good memories. They'd probably beat me at a game of Scrabble.

Ants

They must be quite clever because they can carry things that are much bigger than them. Have you ever looked at what an ant does when you've dropped a bit of a sandwich on the floor? It just picks up a massive crumb and puts it on its back, even though it's about the same size as if I picked up a house and carried it.

Pigeons

They don't look like they should be clever at all but they're good at knowing where they're going because people used to send pigeons to give people messages and they always managed to find their way home again. Someone told me they can remember hundreds of different photos! So ridiculous. They look a bit like rats though, rats with wings.

Dogs

Now dogs are almost like humans but they can't speak. They recognise their owners' faces and they run up to you when they see you. They know TV programmes they like and they answer to their name. They can also be sensitive and get jealous, and if you hurt them they won't forget it for their whole life. So be nice to dogs.

Pigs

They are well clever but I'm not going to talk about them here. You already know my thoughts on pigs (see page 82).

Parrots

They've got voice boxes and know how to sound like humans. They're very colourful and tropical. I like to call them breddas, which means they copy. My mate has a parrot and when you say to it 'Do you want a McDonalds?' it does that whistle noise from the adverts 'Do do do do do... I'm lovin it'. And every time the phone rings it says 'Hello! Hello!'

Rats

They're used in loads of experiments that are meant for humans, so they must be pretty smart... or stupid for letting people experiment on them. They're good at finding shortcuts in experiments designed by mega smart scientists. I think most people hate the look of rats so they haven't given them a chance to prove how clever they are.

Sheep

They always stay together which is clever. So if anyone tries to beat them up they've got back up. They can recognise your face if they've seen you before. It's weird thinking that's a load of woolly jumpers walking down the road. Sheep have got really powerful memories and can tell when one of their mates is lost.

Dolphins

Now these are the best. They've got their own language to communicate with each other and they're just cute, aren't they? They're really friendly and can find their cousins and other relatives in the sea even if they're miles away. Some people reckon bottlenose dolphins can recognise themselves in a mirror too. What are YOU sayin'? No actually, what are YOU looking at?

Elephants

These guys are bigger than most other animals so they *must* just have larger brains. Their brains weigh about 5 kilos. Elephants can use different objects without being taught — so they could pick up a paintbrush and paint a picture! And maybe even a knife and fork.

Chimpanzees

I met the cleverest chimp in the world when I did *Educating Joey Essex* in Africa. I can't remember her name now, was it Sarah? No, I think it was Natasha. But she was much cleverer than me anyway.

DESCRIBE EACH DAY THIS WEEK USING AN EMOJI

Monday:

Tuesday:

Wednesday:

Thursday:

Friday:

Saturday:

Sunday:

Joey's Headscratchers

WHERE DID THE DINOSAURS GO?

Dinosaurs weren't real, were they? Weren't they just in films?
Oh.
To think that dinosaurs were actually here once walking about in
the same places as we do is crazy. KERRRRAZZZY.

Imagine you go to a shop or a restaurant you always like to visit
and then think about how millions of years ago there might have
been a dinosaur standing in that very same spot. Except they
probably weren't in there trying on a pair of shoes like you, or
eating a biscuit. They wouldn't fit into any shoes. And I don't think
they liked biscuits. They preferred eating humans and leaves.

How did they become extinct though? I guess they couldn't survive
in the world because they ran out of decent food. They probably
saw Nando's and decided they wouldn't like peri peri chicken. Too
hot for them to handle.

If I was a dinosaur I'd be a pterodactyl because they can fly, or I'd be a T-Rex because they were the most powerful ones. I used to have loads of dinosaur toys after *Jurassic Park* came out. I loved that film (it would get 10 out of 10). I remember the bit when the dinosaurs were walking about in the kitchen and these humans were hiding.

I'd love to have a dinosaur as a pet, but only if it was a friendly one. I reckon they'd be sick as pets. It really is a shame they're not about anymore. Not the big ones – because they'd try and take over the world – but the baby ones would be well cool.

I'd call it Dave or Bob.

Cavemen are weird too. They're still about apparently. I think they live somewhere in Ibiza. I was in a club there once and someone told me there were cavemen in the mountains. They didn't know how to talk and they probably smelt. I think they were like tramps before tramps existed.

Living in a cave wouldn't be very nice. I think it would be really sore because there wouldn't be any cushions to sit on. Imagine me living in a cave? I would never be able to handle that. I'd be able to handle it if I could have my porridge and some electricity. But I don't think that counts.

Here are some dinosaur facts I've learnt:

They died 65 million years ago
The word dinosaur means 'terrible lizard' in Greek
Velociraptor means 'peedy robber'. Sick!
There were more than 700 different types of dinosaur
Some people think they were killed off by giant waves, others
think it was a big rock from space, and some think it was
volcanoes. But I think maybe they just died of boredom because
they didn't have any TV to watch.

Here's a poem about dinosaurs:

They're pretty fierce
A bit like my mate Tom Pearce
Some of them eat meat
And others just like leaves as a treat
They don't like wearing things on their feet
(mainly because they wouldn't be able to find shoes to fit them)
They were in a film called Jurassic Park
Which some people thought was scarier than the dark
I'd like to have one as a pet
As long as the bills weren't too much at the vet
It's a shame they're not about now
Because they'd be better than having a cow

Buy someone special A BUNCH OF FLOWERS

WHAT WOULD YOU DO IF YOU WERE KING OR QUEEN FOR THE DAY?

If I was king the first thing I would do is make a Twitter account and ring up the government and ask them if I could have my account as @King and I'd get verified the same day. Then I'd do something on Instagram with the same user name and I'd start tweeting and saying, 'I am the king! Who wants a piece of me?'

My number plate would be KING. Everything I owned would say 'King'. I'd change my name from Joey to 'King Essex'.

(Actually I'd better be king for longer than a day otherwise it would be loooong having to change everything back again.)

I'd get a Ferrari straight away and drive about Essex. I'd wear a crown. I'd make a rule so I could knight people. I'd knight my dad first of all, then all my mates. And I'd have my face on all the bank notes.

I'd get my outfit made by a proper designer. I'd be a black, red and silver sort of king ... and I'd have a different colour crown for different moods.

If I was king I suppose a lot of people would want to be queen but I'd choose wisely. I'd go to America or somewhere really cool and take a month or two to find the perfect salty potato. Imagine if the king really did that! People would say 'The king's nuts, mate!'

WHAT WOULD YOU DO?

VACANCY

Do something nice for a stranger today.

WRITE DOWN HOW MANY POKÉMON CHARACTERS YOU CAN REMEMBER

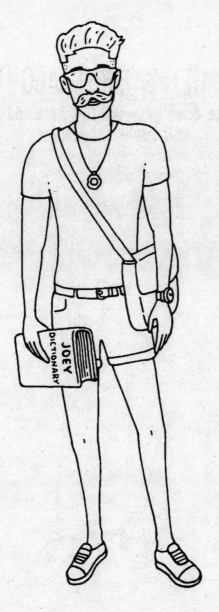

WE ALL GET WORRIED ABOUT STUFF.
Write down your worries here and how you might solve them.

I am worried about:

To solve this I will:

I am worried about:

To solve this I will:

I am worried about:

To solve this I will:

I am worried about:

To solve this I will:

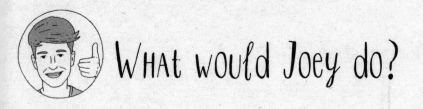

WHAT would Joey do?

Here are some more super strange dilemmas that I've answered. Read the questions and think about your answer before you read what I've said. How different or similar are your answers to mine?

Q: What treatment would you ask for if you were addicted to therapy?

Your answer:

Joey's answer:
I'd want to be able to go back in time for a bit so I'd ask to be given a special flashback cure. I know that doesn't make sense because I haven't got a problem with flashbacks that need a cure but I'd love to time travel so I might as well ask my therapist if I'm paying them anyway.

Q: If you were a geometric shape, what would you like to be?

Your answer:

Joey's answer:
I'd be a circle so I could roll around everywhere. I could be a special Joey wheel.

Q: Do you twist your tongue while saying a tongue twister?

Your answer:

Joey's answer:
I'm quite good at tongue twisters – check me out...

How much wood would a wood chuck chuck if a wood chuck could chuck wood, he would chuck his wood as much as he could if a wood chuck would chuck wood.

I can do it really fast. I had a book with loads of them in and I learnt them. It makes sense to me. I think my tongue probably did a few twists at the time though. There's also the red lorry yellow lorry one and the sea shells on the sea shore. And something about Michelle. Don't know who she is.

Q: If you are to take a picture of cheese, what do you think it would say?

Your answer:

Joey's answer:
If I took a picture of a cheese I reckon the cheese would tell me to piss off. I think cheese would be quite rude if it could talk. I think they're quite hard little things and get a bit moody with humans eating them all the time. Imagine if all food was like a human! Bread would be really lazy and broccoli would be really happy and smiley and bouncy with big white eyes. Carrots would be like the Essex boys of the food world because they look like they've been on sunbeds all the time. And chocolate fingers would be quite ratty and hyperactive because they're full of too much sugar.

SEND SOMEONE A LOVE LETTER

THE JOEY OLYMPICS

I'm now an official champion of sports! Can you believe I won
The Jump on Channel 4? I never imagined I would win in a million
years. No one there could believe it either. It was ledge though. I
now feel like I've really achieved something.

If I had to create an Olympic sport I'd make sure it was in the
snow because I'm good in the snow. But it would have to combine
sport and normal things, like eating your dinner. That's it! My new
sport would be where you'd have to try and eat your dinner going
down a snowy slope. So you'd have a team of you, maybe four or
six people round a table and you'd all have skis on your feet but
the trick would be you'd have to be sliding down the slope while
eating your dinner at the same time and you wouldn't be
able to drop it. You'd have to sit on actual chairs and
it would be a normal dining room table. You'd have to
have eaten all your dinner without spilling it by the
time you get to the bottom of the slope. Team work.

It could be called Skeating – skating and eating.

WHAT WOULD YOU LIKE TO SEE AS AN OLYMPIC SPORT? DESCRIBE IT AND DRAW WHAT IT MIGHT LOOK LIKE.

MY ULTIMATE MIX TAPE
BY JOEY ESSEX

BODY GROOVE - ARCHITECTS FT. NANA

It reminds me of when I was thirten and was in a club in Brentwood partying with Tom Pearce. We played a game to see who could kiss the most girls. So it was literally a body *groooove*.

EVERYBODY FALLS IN LOVE SOMETIMES - TANTO AND DEVONTE

That reminds me of being out with Pixie Lott when I was younger. We used to love that song.

LANGUAGE - DRAKE

I'm not a massive fan of his songs but I think he's a cool guy and I like this one.

BEAUTIFUL SOUL - JESSE MCCARTNEY

Reminds me of being in love with loads of girls, and I wanted to be able to sing like him. It was my old skool love song.

STEAL MY SUNSHINE - LEN

For some reason this reminds me of going to a museum. I think it was a science museum.

LADY - MOJO

This song makes me think of Jamie Oliver. I think it was on one of his programmes once.

I WANNA BE YOUR LOVER - PRINCE

Not to be confused with my cat Prince.

LIFE STYLE - RICH GANG

This song is all about me!

24HRS FT. TWO CHAINS - TEEFLII

Makes me think of Los Angeles partying with the boys.

THINKING OUT LOUD - ED SHEERAN

The perfect song for being with a girl. Ed knows what he's doing.

My mix tape would need a name (so will yours), so I'd like to call it 'A bit of this and bit of that #straight'. People would say 'What's on your mix tape?' and I'd say 'a bit of this and bit of that'.

See what I did there?!

WHAT WOULD BE ON YOUR ULTIMATE MIX TAPE? GO CREATE YOUR PERFECT PLAYLIST.

 Tweet me your suggestion using #Essmix

INVENT YOUR OWN WORDS TO GO INTO THE REEM DICTIONARY.

IF YOU WERE A SUPERHERO WHAT WOULD YOU
LOOK LIKE, WHAT GADGETS WOULD YOU HAVE,
AND WHAT SUPERPOWERS WOULD YOU HAVE?

Draw yourself below.

WHO IS IN YOUR CELEBRITY FAMILY?

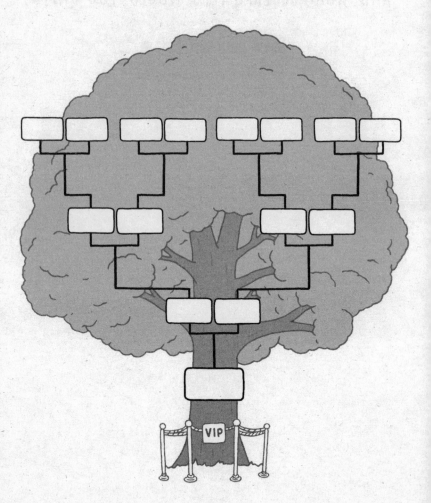

Make breakfast for someone you love.

WRITE THE MENU BELOW.

I LOVE GOING TO THEME PARKS AND RIDING ON SCARY RIDES.

Thorpe Park has loads of good ones. I never get scared on them, why would you? They only last two minutes and then they're over. The best people to go on rides with are girls because then you can flirt with them, and give them a hug if they're frightened. What are YOU sayin'?

I like being scared, I like the rush and the adrenaline.

Visit your local funfair or theme park. Try out five rides and review them here.

Name of the ride:
Description:
Your review:

Star rating:

Name of the ride:
Description:
Your review:

Star rating:

Name of the ride:
Description:
Your review:

Star rating:

Name of the ride:
Description:
Your review:

Star rating:

Name of the ride:
Description:
Your review:

Star rating:

THE JOEY'S
(A BIT LIKE THE OSCARS, BUT MORE CREEPY SICK THAN THAT.)

BEST PERSON TO PARTY WITH

My friend Jake Taylor. He's good at dancing
and is on the same level as me.

BEST HAIR

I'd have to give this to myself. There's no one else who can get
this award. My hair is changing all the time, it's versatile like a
reptile. At the moment I'm calling my hair a 'skinny latte'.

BEST CLOTHES

A$AP Rocky. He's got a good dress sense. He has swag. I was
going to say Pharrell but his hats are too big for his head.

BEST ANIMAL

Squirrel. They're becoming my new favourite now. I'm moving on
from the frog. I like the fact they can crack nuts.

BEST COUPLE

Victoria and David Beckham. No one can beat them. They're the best.

BEST CAR

Lamborghini. I'm going to get one next year, an orange one with my special Essex number plate.

BEST SHOES

Patrick Cox. They're old skool but they're coooool.

BEST AT SELFIES

Justin Bieber. But he always takes pictures of his abs in the gym. I'm going to start doing that soon.

BEST BAR

Nu Bar in Essex. I go there all the time. It's legendary and old skool.

BEST ANGRY PERSON

Charlie Lewis, my friend. Because when he gets angry it's the most non-angry thing I've ever seen.

BEST TAN

Mila Kunis from *Forgetting Sarah Marshall*. She has amazing skin.

BEST FACE

Kylie Jenner.

BEST LEGS

Kendall Jenner. They go on forever.

BEST HANDS

Miley Cyrus has nice long hands.

LEARN HOW TO SAY HELLO IN FIVE DIFFERENT LANGUAGES

JOEY'S DREAM HOUSE

My dream house will have two giant massive gates – one on the left and one on the right, and a big roundabout in the middle. The house will have a medium-sized front door, thick and wooden. It will be a bit like a castle and it has to have three floors and the floors to all be see-through.

Before the house, after the gates, will be a park. Like a mini-festival area with a bar and fake grass. There will be giant speakers because it will be a party place. I'll have about eight bedrooms plus a cinema and a snooker room.

There will be an underground swimming pool and gym – I don't want an outside pool because it looks muddy after a year.

I want a fountain, maybe a statue of my cat Prince and me. And maybe some of my mates can join in the statue – Steve, Tom and James.

I used to want a slide going round the outside from my bedroom but that's not such a good idea because it might look tacky and the rain will make it rusty. So instead I'll have a slide inside from my bedroom to my kitchen. It would go into a ball-pond or something soft for me to land on then I'll get into the chair and eat my breakfast.

I'd have one room totally silver and my toilets would all be different colours — I'd flick a switch and the colour would change in the loo. So every time I do a selfie in the toilet it would look like I was in a different toilet!

WHAT WOULD YOUR DREAM HOUSE LOOK LIKE? DRAW IT BELOW.

WRITE YOUR OWN ENDING TO THESE FAIRYTALES AND NURSERY RHYMES THAT I'VE STARTED.

Jack and Jill went up the hill...

Once upon a time a shoemaker and his wife ran a small shoe store...

One day, Little Red Riding Hood's mother said to her ...

A poor woodcutter and his wife had two children named
Hansel and Gretel ...

Once upon a time there were three little pigs ...

START WRITING YOUR AUTOBIOGRAPHY.

WHAT WOULD IT BE CALLED?

Go and eat fish and chips by the sea.

TAKE A SELFIE WITH A SICK CAR AND PRETEND IT'S YOURS!

WHAT IS YOUR SOAP STAR NAME?

USE YOUR MIDDLE NAME AND THE CITY WHERE YOU WERE BORN

MINE IS DON LONDON...
WHICH IS FUNNY 'COS MY DAD'S
NAME IS DON ESSEX

DRAW THE OUTFIT YOU WOULD WEAR ON A FIRST DATE.

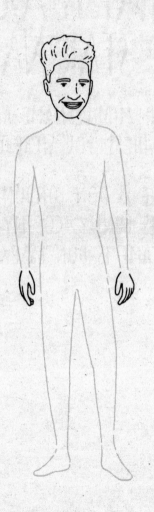

WHAT I BOUGHT TODAY...

What's the most you've ever spent in one day? I've spent £7,000, which is a ridiculous amount. But because I'm so busy all the time I don't get to go to the shops much, so when I do I can get a bit carried away. The reason I spent so much was because I was buying suits and they're probably the most expensive things to buy.

I bought a Gucci suit and only wore it once which was a real waste. I think I thought because it was Gucci it was going to be this amazing fit, but I've had my own suits made-to-measure for me in Dubai now and they're much better than Gucci. I've designed my own. I've made my own line in suits: Essexi. I've got twelve suits all different colours all made for me.

But here's what I bought today:

o Coconut milk
o Bananas
o Digestives
o Sushi
o Tomato sauce

Not quite as cool as suits, but there we go.

WHAT WOULD I TAKE ON A DESERT ISLAND IF I WAS STRANDED?

I'm going to write a list then you need to do yours on the other side of the page:

- O Joey Essex hairspray
- O My Rolex
- O My Fusey teddy bear
- O My speakers so I could plug them into the tree
- O A pair of black skinny jeans
- O My phone
- O Versace sunglasses
- O Lipsalve
- O A bucket hat
- O A suitcase so I don't have to carry it all
- O Some shampoo
- O A game of Twister
- O A fishing rod

IF I WERE STRANDED ON A DESERT ISLAND I WOULD TAKE...

Start a game of Chinese whispers on the bus

IF YOU COULD TRAVEL BACK IN TIME...

WHERE WOULD YOU GO?
WHAT WOULD YOU DO?
WHO WOULD YOU TAKE?

Tell me below.

PUT TOGETHER YOUR PERFECT BAND.

Here's who I would have in the band:

1. ME – JOEY ESSEX
I'd have to put me in the band first of all (obviously). I'd have the biggest part but I wouldn't say much in interviews. I'd be all mysterious. What they call the boat.

2. HARRY STYLES
3. JUSTIN BIEBER
4. TAYLOR SWIFT
5. SELENA GOMEZ
6. CARLY RAE JEPSON

I'd tell Bieber and Harry to 'leave it out' so I could go out with who I wanted in the band. I'd probably date Taylor Swift if I had the choice because she's quite fit and likes a bit of fashion. She's nice to her fans too and gives them advice and stuff and I like that. So the other boys would just have to stand back and wait in line for Joey Essex.

I'd call us Half And Half. Or Surf And Turf.

WHO WOULD BE IN YOUR PERFECT BAND?

My favourite childhood toy

My favourite toy was a silver Buzz Lightyear. I LOVED it. I want one now actually! Can you still buy them? I might have to Google it now and see.

Here's what I remember it looked like...

Buzz
Lightyear!

WHAT DID YOUR FAVOURITE CHILDHOOD TOY LOOK LIKE? DRAW IT ON THIS PAGE.

MAKE A TIME CAPSULE,

fill it with things that you want
someone to find in fifty years' time.
draw what's in it below.

JOEY'S FIRSTS

MY FIRST BIKE...
Was a Dennis the Menace bike.
It had stabilisers and was well sick.

MY FIRST PET...
Was Tiddles my cat. I nearly broke her tail in the patio door
by accident once.

MY FIRST KISS...
Was a girl in primary school. I think she was called Verity.

MY FIRST DATE...
Was with my first serious girlfriend Sidney. We went to an
Italian restaurant.

THE FIRST SONG I BOUGHT...
I used to love Eminem. The one that says something about
your tea going cold, with that Dido woman. What was it called?
'Stan', that's it.

MY FIRST HAIRCUT...
A blond bowl cut.

MY FIRST CAR...
Ford Fiesta.

MY FIRST FIGHT...
Somewhere down near the brook where I used to play when I was younger. I can't remember who it was with though.

MY FIRST HOLIDAY...
Marbella with my dad. But it was a very different Marbella to the one I go to with my mates!

MY FIRST PAIR OF TRAINERS...
Diadora. I'd wear them now, they're still cool.

MY FIRST ALCOHOLIC DRINK...
Vodka lemonade, and I got drunk off one drink!

Try to beat a
Guinness World Record

 Share this on Instagram

Joey's Headscratchers

DOES TIME TRAVEL EXIST?

Surely time travel can't happen unless you freeze yourself?

But you're not actually allowed to freeze yourself yet because
I think it's against the law. You can't freeze yourself unless
you're legally dead but you couldn't be properly dead otherwise
the freezing yourself wouldn't work because you'd be dead. It's
very confusing. So to be legally dead your heart needs to have
stopped, but to be totally properly dead your brain needs to have
stopped too. Or at least that's what I think.

If you're legally dead then a team of special people who you've
ordered to freeze you can come in and keep your blood from
clotting by packing you with ice – a bit like anti-freeze for your
body. Then you get put into some pod thing and filled with liquid
nitrogen and then wait for someone to wake you up and hope they
can get rid of all the ice on you.

Simon Cowell said he read that you could only survive being frozen if it was just your head. So there might be just a load of heads travelling about. Imagine if we just had all our heads chatting to each other!? You wouldn't need any clothes so that would be quite cheap.

If I could travel in time I'd go into the future 500 years and see what was going on, like whether people were using jet packs, and fly about. There would be loads of stuff I'd find out.

I'd also go to Mars and see if there's oxygen there. If there's not I'd come back here and then I'd say 'Can I do that again?' and they'd say 'Go on then, one more time'.

'They' are the time people.

I think I'd be the only person allowed to travel in time because I can't tell the time anyway so it would be perfect for me.

Then I'd travel to the time where the chicken and the egg question happened but I bet it wouldn't be a chicken or an egg... it would be an ant or something.

If you could travel just ten years in the future and were able to use someone's computer – what would you type into Google?

Here's what I'd search for:

I'd find out what the Lottery numbers were for the last ten years and then I'd win loads of money!

I'd look up who I'd been dating so I'd know whether to avoid them or not. Or whether I'd already met the person I was going to marry.

I'd check out what news had been going on so I could help the world. Then when I went back to my time everyone would think I was some mad psychic predictor person who knew the future and I'd be on loads of chat shows as Future Proof Joey.

I'd see what stock had gone up really high and then I'd invest all my Lottery money into that stock.

I'd buy loads and loads of cars with all the money I'd won. So my final Google search would be for the best cars I could find.

Imagine if you could go back in time as well as forward. You could have a little chat with yourself when you were younger. I'd go back to when I was two. But my mind wouldn't be like a two-year-old's, it would be the same mind I have now so I'd know everything that had happened to me but I'd be in a two-year old body. And I'd be able to tell myself how good life was going to get and that I should stop crying over Furbies because when I'm twenty-four I will have enough money to buy as many Furbies as I want.

194

Anyway, if we haven't already been visited by people in the future doesn't that mean that time travel doesn't exist? Because if it did then surely I would have already met my older self...?

My brain hurts.

JOEY DICTIONARY:
PART II

I'm always making up new words for things, and the first
part of this dictionary was in *Being Reem*. Some of them don't
mean anything to anyone else apart from me and my mates.
Here's a few of my latest ones. See if you can drop them into
conversations, and maybe make up a few of your own too and
tweet them to me using the hashtag #JoeyDictionary

WALLOP: means sweet, 'Yeah I'm sick at that – wallop!' You
don't really need to say it, it's just an extra word. Like an
exclamation mark at the end of a sentence. It makes it more
of a powerful word.

ZAGGO: I like Z's at the moment.

ZIG: I like that word too. *Zag zig, zig zag...* I don't know when
I'd use them in a sentence though. Maybe you can decide for
me. There is another word I like with a Z though and that's *zip*
which is a meal that my mate Steve and I make out of couscous,
avocado and onions. I also use it to describe any food that's

196

nice. I'll say 'that's zip' or 'that was a zip dinner'. It saves your breath because it's shorter than saying 'that dinner was nice'.

BREDDA: that means to copy something. So if you're a bredda that's like you're a parrot.

CRYSTALLISED: which means 'That's a really really pretty day', meaning it's a crystallised day.

PROPER CHOOOOOOUUNNNG: the flavouring of something good – that smells chooooounnng. Like candles.

MINERALS: you've got minerals means you've got good game.

RANGING: this is the word for when you're in a busy club and you keep your head down and move through the crowd like a worm.

G: means gangsta. You are so G means you are so cool.

Try and use some of these this week!

DRAW YOUR LIFE STORY...

WRITE A NOTE TO YOUR FRIEND USING INVISIBLE INK

Here's how to do it:

Put lemon juice in bowl. Dip a cotton bud in the lemon juice. Using milk, vinegar, or orange juice instead of lemon juice will have the same effect.

Write your message...

You can use a paintbrush or a toothpick instead of a cotton bud.

Tell your mate to heat the paper... like on a radiator.

Your secret message will appear. Like MAGIC!

QUESTION:

HOW MANY HELIUM BALLOONS WOULD IT TAKE TO LIFT JOEY ESSEX OFF THE GROUND?...

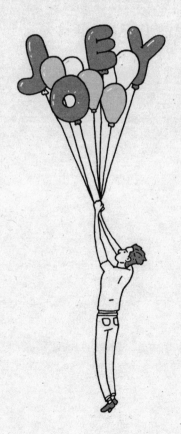

*Answer on page 272

Design your own car.

DRAW IT BELOW

WRITE THE FIRST THING THAT JUMPS INTO YOUR HEAD AFTER READING THESE WORDS...

Frog —

Lightning —

Reem —

Joey —

Sugar —

Lion —

River —

Chair —

Bucket —

Boat —

JOEY'S DREAM DIARY

Apparently the stuff you dream about can mean certain things are going to happen to you. There are loads of things on the internet and people have written books about what dreams mean... there are even dream dictionaries. Which sound a bit rubbish to me.

Here are a few things that I've dreamt about recently and what I think they mean – plus what the dream makers say they mean. See which ones you think are better!

FALLING

JOEY'S INTERPRETATION:
You're about to lose one of your legs. That's why you keep falling over.

DREAM DICTIONARY:
You're worried about something and lack confidence in some area of your life. You're worried about letting go of something.

LOSING YOUR TEETH

JOEY'S INTERPRETATION:
You haven't cleaned your teeth properly. I clean mine about five times a day. So I never dream I'm losing my teeth.

DREAM DICTIONARY:
Dreaming about teeth falling out symbolises change or the fear of losing something important.

HAVING A BABY

JOEY'S INTERPRETATION:
You've gone a bit mad.

DREAM DICTIONARY:
You are looking forward to new beginnings. And all you want is to be happy.

KANGAROO

JOEY'S INTERPRETATION:
You need to renew your zoo membership.

DREAM DICTIONARY:
Kangaroos can jump around so it might be that you're worried about something you can't connect with.

EYELASHES

JOEY'S INTERPRETATION:
You've been reading too many women's magazines.

DREAM DICTIONARY:
If you dream your eyelashes are falling out this symbolises you're worried you're becoming less attractive. If you dream you're putting make-up on then you're trying to increase your appeal to others.

WATERFALL

JOEY'S INTERPRETATION:
You're thirsty.

DREAM DICTIONARY:
Dreaming of a waterfall is a great dream symbol. It means cleansing and new beginnings.

PLAY A GAME OF CONSEQUENCES BY TEARING OUT THIS PAGE

TRY DRAWING A HAND
WITH YOUR EYES SHUT

DESIGN YOUR OWN PAIR OF TRAINERS.

DRAW ON THE TRAINERS BELOW:

DRAW THE THINNEST NOSE YOU CAN MANAGE.
I'VE ATTEMPTED 3 THIN NOSES.

THIS IS MY BEST EFFORT.

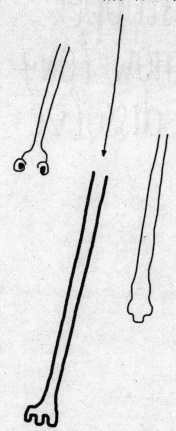

Eat a Gobstopper and time how long it takes to dissolve

WRITE YOUR FIVE-YEAR PLAN

COME UP WITH AN INVENTION

...LIKE ON *DRAGON'S DEN*.

DRAW IT BELOW, WRITE WHAT IT DOES AND
THEN PITCH IT TO YOUR FRIENDS AND FAMILY.

What I'm Grateful For
BY JOEY ESSEX

- My family
- Friends
- Porridge
- My bed
- My shower
- Toothpaste
- My mobile phone
- Twitter
- Fit girls
- Living in Essex
- My hair
- Socks
- Being able to jump so I could win The Jump.

Joey's Headscratchers

ARE SUPERHEROES REAL?

I like to think that superheroes could be real. Mainly because I want to be one when I'm older. I'd be able to hover. I'd never bother walking anywhere so I'd probably end up getting really fat – I'd hover into a club or down the road. I'd be able to ask people to move out of my way without speaking to them – I'd have amazing powers of mind control.

My main ability (as well as being able to hover) would be to read someone's mind – it probably wouldn't do me any favours but it would be the best power in the world. If I could read girls' minds I reckon they'd be thinking 'I want to talk to him but I don't know if he wants to talk to me'... when really I do want them to talk to me. I think girls get quite worried about stuff and I think they get scared to talk to me. And I don't think like that. They think I'm someone different but I'm not and that's quite frustrating...

If I was a superhero then I'd make sure my hair could change whenever I wanted. I'd cut my hair and then click fingers and it would stop growing. I hate getting my hair cut all the time. But this way, if I wanted to see what it was like long I could just 'click'. I could choose one from Google and have whatever I wanted.

I'd have a cape and a jet pack.

What would I be called? I like the name ZED but backwards it would be DEZ.

ZED man.

It would be like Superman and Clark Kent — so I'd be called 'Dezzer' when I'm on my days off being a superhero.

Here are some other superheroes I think should exist:

Plastic man

He's a human made out of plastic. If something broke all he'd need to do is buy a new part for his body.

Microwave man

A human being made with a microwave head. Everyone would want him around all the time because he'd be able to feed them when they were hungry. He'd always make a silly pinging noise though so he wouldn't be able to hide the fact he was coming.

Woodman

No one would like him because he'd be too boring and wooden for any conversations.

Ironman

Only this wouldn't be the ironman you know from the films. This would be someone with an actual iron on his head. So he'd always have really neat shirts but his head would be very flat and hot.

Toothman

He would dazzle you with his extra white smile.

Carrot man

He would be able to see in the dark because he ate so many carrots. (Why do people say that actually? How the hell can a carrot help you see in the dark?) He'd also look like he'd been on holiday and everyone would be jealous of his orange glow.

Duckman

He would have secret powers on the water.

There are some actual real life humans with powers we didn't even know existed. I've been reading about them. Check these out:

Daniel Paul Tammet is a British man with the biggest brain in the world. He can memorise pretty much anything and can learn any language really quickly. He did it for a Channel 5 documentary and learnt how to speak Icelandic in seven days. At the end of it his instructor said he was 'Not human'. If I had a teacher they'd say the same to me but it would be for the opposite reason – because I hadn't been able to learn a thing!

Ben Underwood is a boy who can see things even though he's blind. He's from America and had cancer so had to have his eyes removed but he can play basketball, ride bikes and he just uses sound. He makes a clicking sound and can tell how far things are away from the way the sound bounces off objects. He's like a human dolphin (they use sound to work out locations too).

The Rubberboy is a man who's got five Guinness world records for being the most flexible man alive. His real name is Daniel Browning Smith and he can dislocate his arms to crawl through an unstrung tennis raquet. He's been on loads of US TV shows because no one can quite believe what they're seeing.

Monsieur Mangetout which is French for Mr Eat it all. A guy called Michel Lotito who can eat anything – metal, rubber, bikes, TVs. He even ate a whole airplane once – it took him two years from 1978 to 1980.

King Tooth is a guy from Malaysia called Raja Gigi and he pulled a train with just his teeth in 2007. The train had six coaches attached and weighed 297.1 tonnes!

SNOG MARRY AVOID

Dot Cotton from *EastEnders*, Rita from *Coronation Street*, Julie Walters

I don't know who any of them are. Who's the fittest? I'll have a stab in the dark and say 'Marry Rita, snog Julie and avoid Dot' because she smokes. And I don't like fags.

Kim Kardashian, Khloé Kardashian, Kourtney Kardashian

Marry Kourtney … she's the fittest out of them. I'd avoid Khloé because she's too tall for me. I think Kim's gone a bit nuts lately anyway and keeps getting her bits out in magazines. But I don't think she can lose really because everything she does is crazy.

Holly Willoughby, Fearne Cotton, Emma Willis

I really quite fancy Fearne Cotton at the moment so I'd marry her. I'd snog Holly and I'd have to avoid Emma. Although she's a sort too. This is a hard one!

Meghan Trainor, Ellie Goulding, Tulisa

Avoid Meghan Trainor, marry Ellie and snog Tulisa.

Katie Hopkins, Katie Price, Mel B

I'd marry Katie Price and be another one of the husbands on her bed post. I'd snog Mel B even though she'd probably eat me alive and bite my face. I'd have to avoid Katie Hopkins.

Gemma Collins, Carol Wright, Nanny Pat

Marry Nanny Pat, snog Gemma and avoid Carol. Sorry Carol, bit of a liberty there...!

Cheryl Fernandez-Versini, Victoria Beckham, Abbey Clancy

Marry Victoria Beckham, snog Abbey and avoid Cheryl. Or can I just snog all of them?

Vicky Pattison from *Geordie Shore*, Casey Batchelor, Charlotte Crosby from *Geordie Shore*

Marry Charlotte, snog Vicky and avoid Casey.

Lucy Watson, Binky, Millie Mackintosh

Avoid Millie, snog Lucy and marry Binky.

KEEP A NOTE OF YOUR
TOP TENS

My top ten favourite books:

My top ten items of clothing I own:

My top ten favourite animals:

My top ten best birthday presents:

My top ten favourite songs:

My top ten favourite films:

My top ten favourite quotes:

My top ten days or nights out:

JOEY'S TOP TENS

SWEETS

- Haribo
- Milk bottles
- Coca cola bottles
- Cherry drops
- Chewits
- Brain Lickers
- Toxic Waste
- Skittles – to make you go crazy
- Sherbert lemons
- Fruit pastels

SNACKS

- Cheese and onion crisps
- Toast with Marmite
- Beans on toast with cheese on top
- Salt beef bagel
- Sausage roll
- Nutella on toast with bananas
- Pancakes

- Bacon and cheese pasty
- Pizza
- Pickled onion Monster Munch

TV SHOWS
- TOWIE
- Educating Joey Essex
- I'm a Celebrity ... Get Me Out of Here!
- Celebrity Juice
- The Keith Lemon Sketch Show
- Made in Chelsea
- Keeping Up with the Kardashians
- Newsnight (only joking)
- The Cube
- South Park

THINGS IN MY WARDROBE
- A big Louis Vuitton bag
- Moncler boots
- A Fusey T-shirt
- Odd socks
- A Chanel scarf
- A woolly hat
- Dr Martens boots
- A red and black jumper
- A suit
- A tie

IN MY FRIDGE

- Coconut milk
- A Dairy Milk chocolate bar
- Spinach
- Tomato sauce
- Sweet potato mash
- Blueberries
- Butter
- Champagne
- Horseradish
- Udo Oil

FESTIVALS

- V Festival
- Lovebox
- Party in the Park
- Glastonbury
- We are FSTVL
- Secret Garden Party
- Wilderness
- Parklife
- T in the Park
- The Joey Essex Festival – that will be NAUGHTY

BAD HABITS

- Biting nails
- Leaving the toilet seat up

- Leaving the front room messy
- Picking my nose
- Sniffing my fingers
- Putting my hands down my trousers when I'm talking to people
- Not replying to people's texts
- Not dusting my TV so I can't actually see it because there's so much dust on it
- Not cleaning my car
- Not giving Prince enough cuddles.

WHAT'S YOUR ULTIMATE TOP TEN

-
-
-
-
-
-
-
-
-
-

HOW MANY SWEETS ARE IN THIS JAR?

*Answer on page 272

Write the lyrics to your own song.

MY FANTASY FILM

If there was a film about my life it would be sick. I'd make
sure I had these people in it: me (obviously), Leonardo DiCaprio,
Rhianna, Justin Bieber and Michael Jordan.

The film would be set in Ibiza and would be designed to show
the world how magical Ibiza is. My character Joey Essex would
own the whole island and everyone would be really jealous of me
because I could buy anything I wanted. I'd then decide to buy
another island called England too.

Leonardo would be my boat driver and Rhianna would be my
personal singer for whenever I felt like I wanted a song. Justin
Bieber would be my chef, even though I'm not sure if he can cook.

I'd probably learn to fly at the end of the film and because Ibiza
is so magical I'd develop some magical powers and could heal
everyone of all their illnesses so they're free to party on the
island for the rest of their lives.

The End.

NOW YOU MAKE UP YOUR DREAM FILM
AND WHO WOULD PLAY YOU. MAYBE
I CAN BE IN YOUR FILM TOO?

JOEY WORD ASSOCIATION

Here's a funny way of testing how your brain works. Get one of your mates to say a word and you have to say the first thing that comes into your head that has something to do with that word. Or you can play it by looking at the words here and adding yours in place of the ones my friend put...

WE SAID – hair
JOEY SAID – shampoo

WE SAID – shower
JOEY SAID – ducks

WE SAID – frogs
JOEY SAID – slimey

WE SAID – snail
JOEY SAID – slow

WE SAID – tortoise
JOEY SAID – pop (they pop their heads out)

WE SAID – corn
JOEY SAID – flakes

WE SAID – dandruff
JOEY SAID – dirty

WE SAID – tramp
JOEY SAID – skint

WE SAID – bank
JOEY SAID – cash

Why are we playing this game?!

Go rollerblading in the park

WRITE DOWN TEN THINGS YOU ARE GRATEFUL FOR...

WOULD YOU RATHER...?

See if you answer the questions the same as me... try not to look at my answers before you give yours.

Have no teeth or no hair?
YOUR ANSWER:

JOEY ANSWER:
No hair because without teeth you'd look well dirty.

Would you rather have a head the size of a tennis ball or the size of a watermelon?
YOUR ANSWER:

JOEY ANSWER:
I'd have a head the size of a melon – imagine having a tennis ball head! It would be sooo small.

Would you rather have no penis or five penises?
YOUR ANSWER:

JOEY ANSWER:
Someone asked me once whether I'd rather have a fanny on my forehead or loads of willies on my back. I said I'd rather have the willies on my back because at least then you could cover them up with clothes. I wouldn't go round telling people I had five willies either.

Would you rather peel all your nails out of your fingers or pull all the teeth out of your mouth?
YOUR ANSWER:

JOEY ANSWER:
I like my teeth too much so it would have to be my nails.
Sorry nails.

Would you rather freeze to death or burn to death?
YOUR ANSWER:

JOEY ANSWER:
Freeze.

Would you rather have knives for fingers or penises for fingers?
YOUR ANSWER:

JOEY ANSWER:
Another willy question there! I'd rather have knives for fingers – people would call me Joey Sharp Fingers.

Would you rather have an animal best friend that could be any animal you choose and it would be intelligent and speak to you (and you could ride it around town if it is a large animal like a bear) or be married to someone with a hot body?
YOUR ANSWER:

JOEY ANSWER:
I'd love to have an animal I could chat to but I'd have to choose the hot body.

Would you rather have unlimited love or unlimited money?
YOUR ANSWER:

JOEY ANSWER:
Money. I would usually say love but I wouldn't want to be in love forever since I was one. That would be pretty intense.

Would you rather have horrible acne that is only on areas that are covered with clothing or moderate acne that's only on your face?
YOUR ANSWER:

JOEY ANSWER:
I'd choose it on my face. I wouldn't want it all over my body. I'd get some Clearasil and bath in it until it went away. Or I'd just wear a mask.

Would you rather... Speak any language fluently? Or be able to talk to animals?
YOUR ANSWER:

JOEY ANSWER:
I'd talk to animals. How sick would that be? I'd like to chat to a leopard and a chihuahua.

Would you rather eat a pinecone? Or poop a pinecone?
YOUR ANSWER:

JOEY ANSWER:
Eat one!

Would you rather change gender every time you sneeze? Or not be able to tell the difference between a muffin and a baby?
YOUR ANSWER:

JOEY ANSWER:
Muffin baby! I'd hate to turn into a woman every time I got a cold.

TRY AND SPOT SOME CONSTELLATIONS (PATTERNS OF STARS) IN THE SKY TONIGHT.

Tick off the ones you see...

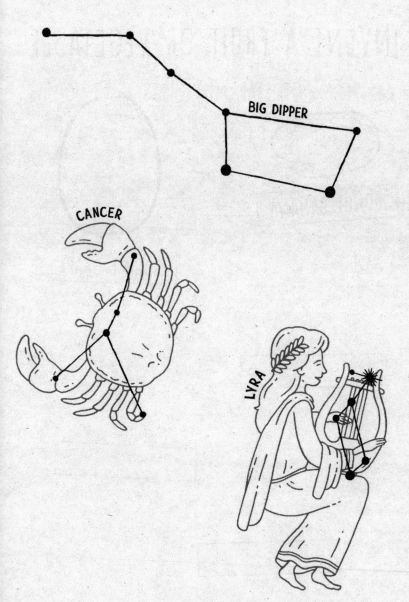

BIG DIPPER

CANCER

LYRA

INVENT A FRUIT OR VEGETABLE

DONUT BANANA

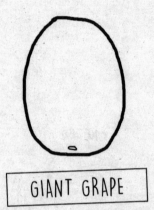

GIANT GRAPE

WHAT WOULD YOU DO IF YOU WON THE LOTTERY?

Write or draw it below.

HOW TO LIVE OFF A BUDGET OF £5 PER DAY

How many times have you been to the shop and not even checked how much things cost before you got to the till? I've done that loads of times before. But if someone told you you had to survive on just £5 then what would you do? You'd definitely need to look at the labels otherwise you'd look like a right idiot when you told the shopkeeper you didn't have enough money and had to put stuff back after you got to the till.

Here's what I reckon you could eat if you had to survive on £5 ...

Breakfast

I don't know how I'd survive without my porridge but a whole box of oats costs £1.70 so my first move would be to knock on the neighbours' door and ask if they can lend me a cup (until I'm not on this budget thing anymore).

Otherwise ... a piece of toast. A loaf of bread from Sainsbury's costs about 40p which could last a whole week.

Snack

A banana to give you energy like a monkey [68p].

Lunch

A ham sandwich [£1.50 for 5 slices of ham] with some lettuce in [60p].

Dinner

A two-egg omelette [£1.25 for 6 eggs] with more of that nice ham and some tomatoes [£1.00 for about 20 cherry ones].

DONE!

WHAT WOULD YOU DO IF YOU HAD AN ALIEN FOR A FRIEND FOR THE DAY?

For a start: how cool would that be?!

I'd love to be able to spend the day with an extraterrestrial. But I reckon I'd want more than a day because there would be so much to do and talk about. If they could talk. They probably couldn't. They'd just look at you weirdly and think you were mad.

If one came to visit me for the day I'd call him Freddo. Because that was the name of one of my favourite chocolate frogs when I was younger. And I reckon he would remind me of a frog.

The first thing I'd do is dress him in one of my Fusey tracksuits. Then I'd take him to Westfield shopping centre to have a look about and see what other outfits he might like.

I'd also take him to the phone shop so he could get a phone and phone home. And I'd ask for his number so we could chat once he had to go back to space.

I wouldn't tell any of my mates about him to start with, I'd keep him a secret for a little bit.

And I'd take him to a KFC for some food but I'd tell him he could take the batter off the chicken first because it might be too greasy for him.

In the evening we'd probably go to Nu Bar in Essex but I'd have to make sure he could dance first. Maybe he'd never heard any music before?! How mad would that be?

Then he'd go home and I'd go and visit him next time. As long as no one ate me once I got to space.

WHAT WOULD YOU DO?

QUICK FIRE QUESTIONS

○ Boiled or fried eggs?
Fried, they taste better.

○ Last person you kissed?
My cat Prince. But I got fur on my face.

○ What's the worst song on your iPod?
Best song ever by One Direction, but it isn't, is it? Because
it's the best one! Actually the worst one is probably *Genie in a
bottle* by Christina Aguilera. And the one that goes... *'Oh what
a night'*. The thing is I never know when it's going to come on
shuffle, it's like gambling.

○ Twitter or Instagram?
Twitter because I've got more followers.

○ What is the first thing you think of when you wake up in the
morning?
Porridge.

O If you could eat lunch with one famous person, who would it be?
  Jim Carrey and I'd say to him 'Can we do another *Ace Ventura: Pet Detective* but can I be in it?'

O What's the last text message you received?
  Steve-o from *Jackass* said, 'Are you feeling better today?'

O Which store would you choose to max out your credit card?
  Versace Versace ... or maybe Chanel.

O What time is bedtime?
  Midnight. I'm worried I'll turn into an owl.

O What did you get for your last birthday?
  A frying pan from my dad. But I don't fry things much anymore.
  So I just look at it sometimes.

O Is the glass half empty or half full?
  Half full. What does that actually mean? What do you mean when
  some people say they're a 'glass half empty kind of person'?
  I think that means you're a bit weird. And a 'glass half full
  person' means you're really, really weird. Apparently it just
  means you're an optimistic person but I feel like I'm a negative
  person towards things ... but I'd still say it was half full.
  Is that a good thing? Good.

○ What's the farthest-away place you've been?
Patagonia. I'd never go back in a million years.

○ Have you ever won a trophy?
I won a football trophy but everyone else got one as well,
about 300 other people!

○ Are you a good cook?
I'm good at cooking breakfast – sausage, beans, bacon,
mushrooms, brown toast... in my dad's frying pan.

○ What was the name of your first pet?
I had two turtles called Cookie and Crumble.

○ Is there anything going on this weekend?
My little mate Danny Walia is coming out with me, we're going
to have a right laugh, I can't wait.

○ How are you feeling right now?
Really achy. I've been doing too much exercise and my arms
are hurting. I should have a bath but I can't be bothered.

○ What is the last movie that you saw at the cinema?
Dumb and Dumber To.

○ Do you sing in the shower?
Yeah. I sing about things I'm doing that day like *'I'm going to*

the shopppp, to the ITV building with friends, we're gonna have a really good time...' I rap about what I'm doing.

O What do you do most when you are bored?
I go Instagram or Twitter. Text my mates, text a girl... or if I'm really really *really* bored I'll text ten girls.

O What are your best physical features?
My eyebrows are quite cool.

O What are your best characteristics?
Carroteristics? Like about carrots? Oh about me... I like the fact I wear skin-tight outfits.

O Are you a morning person or a night owl?
I'm a night owl. I should get an owl tattoo but Justin Bieber has one, hasn't he?

O Can you touch your nose with your tongue?
I've just tried and no!

O Can you close your eyes and raise your eyebrows?
Yes. YEAH!

O How many rings before you answer the phone?
Three.

○ What is your best childhood memory?
  Driving down hills on a Go Cart from Toys R Us when I was ten.

○ Do you worry about your weight?
  I do and I don't. I don't want to get big but I eat quite a lot.
  And at the moment I'm trying to put on muscle.

○ What's the last thing you ate?
  Apple strudel.

○ When did you last take a 'selfie'?
  Last night, in a floppy hat.

○ What does Simon Cowell smell like?
  He doesn't smell as good as me. Like chocolate I reckon.

○ How many pints can you drink before you fall over?
  Probably about ten.

○ How comfy is your bed?
  My bed at home is really comfortable, all bouncy like a cloud.

○ Lipstick or lip gloss?
  Lip gloss — lipstick smudges all over your face!

○ White wine or red wine?
  Red wine, it's healthier and white wine makes people evil.

○ Snog or kiss?
Snog.

○ What's your favourite cheese?
Cheddar – pure cheddar. Only the mild kind though. I don't like
mature. It's too old.

○ Describe what you look like naked in three words.
Chooooounngggg, leaning and 'on point'.

○ Most embarrassing thing you've ever done?
When I was little I dropped a toy down the loo and tried to get
it but my head got stuck.

○ Last person you shouted at?
My mate Danny Walia. I asked him to get me a coat from
Harrods and he called me and said he got me a large. And I
didn't want a large. I feel really bad for shouting. It turned
out it wasn't a large anyway – it was a size 38 which was the
one I needed. So that was a wasted shout.

○ What's the last thing that made you cry?
I burnt my tongue on a cup of tea.

○ What are you like in a fight?
Really good. Very accurate.

CREATE YOUR OWN SHOP.

What is it called?
What does it sell?
Draw it below...

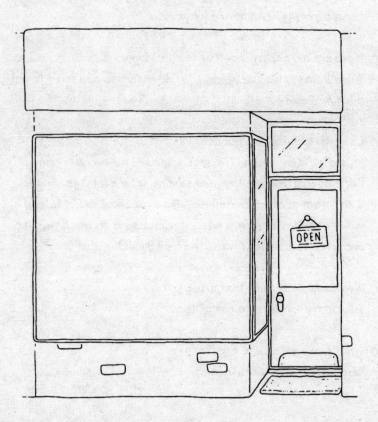

Go and climb a tree

DO A 5000-PIECE JIGSAW PUZZLE

Make a cake that looks like your face

 Tweet your picture at #CakeFace

START A PRANK WAR WITH YOUR MATES.

Play chubby bunny!

TWEET OF THE DAY

Believe it or not there are some people who think of tweets and Twitter as just things that come from the trees. These people are called 'bird spotters' and probably don't have any Twitter followers at all. They've probably never sent a tweet, they just think a tweet is the noise a bird makes.

Bird spotters are weird. They try and find pigeons and stuff. They spend their whole lives doing it! I think you can tell a bird spotter from a mile off because they would always be bumping into the trees and they look a bit trampy, like a pigeon.

Some birds have funny names – like 'blue tit'. That used to make me laugh when I was younger because I thought it was rude.

I wonder if birds can chat to each other using their beaks? Do you think they can understand what we say or does our chat sound like twittery noise to them in the same way their tweeting sounds to us?

Here are some bird facts for you. Just in case you want to tweet any of these one day.

○ The biggest bird in the world is the ostrich, which can grow up to 9 feet tall.

○ A flamingo can eat only when its head is upside down.

○ The longest recorded flight of a chicken is 13 seconds.

○ The bones of a pigeon weigh less than its feathers.

○ A woodpecker can peck twenty times a second.

○ Flamingos are not naturally pink. They get their colour from their food – tiny green algae that turn pink during digestion. Imagine if we changed colour depending on what we ate! I'd be green like broccoli.

○ An albatross can sleep while it flies. It apparently dozes while cruising at 25 mph.

- Penguins can jump as high as 6 feet in the air.

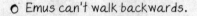

- A chicken with red earlobes will produce brown eggs, and a chicken with white earlobes will produce white eggs.

- Emus can't walk backwards.

- Birds don't sweat.

- Emus run after rain clouds, hoping for water.

- Puffins have teeth that point backwards inside their beaks.

- Emperor penguins breed in colonies scattered around the Antarctic continent.

- Snowy owls can almost turn their heads in a complete circle.

Learn how to say goodbye in five different languages

Joey's Headscratchers

WHO ARE THE MOST IMPORTANT PEOPLE IN HISTORY?

I'm not very good at history and don't really know who many people are, but I'm going to give it a go.

Who was Henry VIII?

He had eight wives' didn't he? And he hated them all so he chopped off all their heads. They were bitches.

Oh he had six wives apparently. Well that's nearly the same as eight.

He had a massive ginger beard and used to eat a lot of food. In my head he looks like the man from Toby Carvery.

I wouldn't want to go and meet him.

He looks scary, and many people were scared of him. I reckon if he didn't get his way, he got cross. And if you made him cross he just chopped off your head.

264

The Beatles

I can never remember their names ... one of them was called
John but what about the rest?

Ashley?

Billy?

Greg?

[Their real names were John, Paul, Ringo and George]

They always dressed in black and white with skinny ties. I quite
like their outfits, Harry Styles looks a bit like them. Did they come
from London? Oh, no ... it was Liverpool, was it?

They were the biggest band in the world way before One Direction.
Everyone was mad for them. There was a guy called Paul McCartney
who was married to Heather Mills who I was in *The Jump* with.

John was the one who got shot apparently but I always get him
mixed up with Paul.

Harry Houdini

I haven't got a clue who he was. But someone told me he used to
escape from loads of places. Cool name anyway. I'd like to be
called Joey Houdini.

Albert Einstein

He's literally Mr Clever Tits. He's an old man with glasses and he
was dyslexic. He was the cleverest man in the world. People say

'Einstein' as if it's a word for 'genius'. He came up with the theory of relativity but I don't think that was to do with who your cousin was. It was much deeper than that.

Nelson Mandela

Was he a singer?
Oh.
No he wasn't apparently.

He's important because he was the first black president of South Africa. And he spent ages in prison for sticking up for human rights and racism. Loads of people loved him. And I think he met the Spice Girls once.

Winston Churchill

Was he from Essex?

Florence Nightingale

Was she a prime minister once?

Charles Dickens

He's definitely from Essex, isn't he? I used to think he lived in Buckingham Palace but he's not a royal. He's a writer.

William Shakespeare

He wrote that story about the boy and the girl. Adam and Eve? Oh I know, Romeo and Juliet. That's it.

DO SOMETHING TODAY
THAT SCARES YOU!

FAN ART GALLERY

Share this with me and your mates on Instagram

THE END

So that's it, we've come to the end of my book. What did you think? Weird or good? Mad or bad? This is one of the most random but exciting books to have been made in the history of the world. It's all about you and I, and I and YOU.

I hope you've had fun writing in it because this has been about both of us making the book together. Don't forget to send me pictures and use the hashtags that I've given you.

It's sad thinking this is the end of the book. End sounds a bit like bend. I hope it hasn't driven you round the bend.

I thought I'd end the book with a bit of a list of rules for life.

My A – Z on what to do if you want to live your life to the full.

Maybe you can do your own A – Z next to mine and see how different your answers are.

A – is for aliens, if you're lucky enough to meet them and hang out with them for the day.

B – for burger but if you don't want to get fat then don't eat the bun.

C – character. You need to have a good one if you're to have a good life.

D – dignity. This makes a person very special.

E – eggs. But don't eat too many. Maybe four but no yolk. And you also might find out what came first – the chicken or the egg?

F – feelings. You need to have them otherwise you'll be an alien.

G – you should be a G. A gangsta.

H – hyper and happy. If you're both then people will like your company.

I – you need these to see.

J – j is for Joey.

K – king. You should dream of being one.

L – losing. You have to lose to be able to win in life.

M – mad. You need to be a bit mad to survive.

N – naughty. This means being a rascal but in a good way.

O – oven. Which I need to cook all my food.

P – Prince my cat. I can't not mention him.

Q – the queen. Who will one day be my mate.

R – rectangle. Just because I like that shape.

S – strong. Be as strong as you can in life.

T – tattoo. Someone is going to design me my first one in this book!

U – underdog. I was the underdog in *The Jump* and I still won. So underdogs can win!

V – victory.

W – winning. Which is the same as victory but never mind.

X – X ray or Joey Esse X. And it's rare to have an X in your name.

Y – why are you so cool?

Z – zebra. Because I like their stripes.

*Loads, obviously!